This book is intended for anyone who is interested in natural history, or simply curious about the world in general, whether or not his special interest is in birds.

The book is an account of the behavior of a number of birds of the American tropical forest, from field studies made by Dr. Snow and his wife in Trinidad, Guyana, and other parts of South and Central America. Some personal details are also given of the circumstances under which the studies were made.

To illustrate the profound evolutionary paths available in this habitat, the author has focused on the fruit-eating birds whose dietary requirements are easily met by the abundance of vegetation. This fact has been associated with the evolution of extreme sexual dimorphism and of the most elaborate and bizarre courtship displays known in birds. Freed from the time-consuming food gathering process by the availability of fruits, the males spend all their time in competitive display and have nothing to do with the nests. Display grounds are often traditional and are used year after year as long as the forest is undisturbed.

These New World equivalents of the birds of paradise of the New Guinea region include the bellbirds, the cock-of-the-rock, and several species of manakins. One specialized fruit-eating bird is included whose evolution has taken a totally different course, the oil-bird. The reasons why it has done so throw light on the factors determining the evolution of the others.

In addition to the accounts of the various species, special chapters are devoted to exploring the "web of adaptation" by which a species is fitted to life in the tropical forest. The adaptations concern not only food but nests, social relations, territory, and escape from predators. It is shown that no aspect of the natural history of a species can be understood in isolation; all are part of a complex interdependent web.

This fascinating book concludes with a powerful, compelling argument for the preservation and conservation of one of the earth's most complex environments.

THE WEB OF

Bird Studies

A Demeter Press Book

ADAPTATION

in the American Tropics

by DAVID W. SNOW

Quadrangle / *The New York Times Book Co.*

Designed by Tere LoPrete

Library of Congress Cataloging in Publication Data

Snow, David William.
    The web of adaptation.

    "A Demeter Press book."
    Includes bibliographical references.
        1. Birds—Tropics.   2. Birds—Latin America.
    3. Adaptation (Biology)   4. Frugivores.   5. Birds—
    Behavior.   I. Title.
    QL695.5.S63   1976   598.2'98   75-24891
    ISBN 0-8129-0603-9

Contents

Introduction

Popular writers would have us think of tropical forests as the scene of the most intense struggle for existence, a riot of different forms of animal life, eating and being eaten, and of plant life, strangling, suffocating, and crowding each other out as they struggle up toward the light. At the other extreme, some who have been impressed by the wealth of beautiful and bizarre animals and plants have pictured tropical forests as a place where life is so easy and food so plentiful that the most extravagant forms of life can develop unchecked.

The truth, so far as we can see it, is somewhere between these two over-simplified extremes. The popular idea certainly has some validity: the impact of predators, and competition with other species for the various resources of food and shelter, have over the millennia forced the animals and plants of the forest along lines of increasing specialization, so that each species occupies its own limited "niche" in the immensely complex forest system, a niche that it can exploit and in which it can survive better than its neighbors. But for birds at any rate, there is also some truth in the other view. Once a bird has survived the dangerous early weeks of life, the tropical forest is a much safer place to live in than the woods of temperate regions. Crises are rare; day after day passes in a peaceful, almost monotonous routine. The contradiction between these two views is in fact more apparent than real: it depends on the time scale that one is adopting. Over the decades and centuries the struggle is intense; but daily life is comparatively peaceful, at least for those individuals that have established themselves in their proper place within the system.

However this may be, there is no doubt that specialization is one of the outstanding features of the birds and other animals of the tropical forest. Birds of temperate latitudes are, by and large, generalists; they have to be in order to survive in a constantly changing environment. Birds of tropical forests, the richest and most unchanging of terrestrial habitats, are specialists; the environment enables them to be, and competitors force them to be. One main line of specialization has led to the evolution of birds that feed mainly on fruit, for obvious reasons an impossible staple diet for birds of temperate latitudes where fruit production is strongly seasonal.

Fruit-eating birds are of two kinds, and the distinction between them is most important. Some eat the fleshy parts of the fruit, the parts that the plant offers to the bird in exchange for the service of distributing the seed. These may be called the "legitimate" fruit-eaters. Other birds take the fruits in order to eat the seeds. Many parrots do this, and some pigeons and other birds; they have, as it were, broken into the mutually beneficial system evolved by the plant and the legitimate fruit-eaters. The unfortunate consequences for man of eating forbidden fruit are well known, but ecologists have yet to explore thoroughly the consequences of the parrots' exploitation of a food supply that was not evolved for their benefit. The evolutionary consequences of legitimate fruit eating are just beginning to be appreciated; they are a main theme of this book.

The most important of these consequences depend on the fact that, to put it anthropomorphically, the fruit "wants" to be eaten. The more of it that the plant produces, and the more attractive it makes its fruit, the more widely will its seeds be dispersed and the more likely it will be to propagate itself. And so such fruit tends to be abundant and conspicuous, and a fruit-eating bird may need to devote a very short period each day to foraging. If the fruit becomes very nutritious, providing enough fats and proteins to nourish not only the adult bird but also its growing young, the fruit-eater may become quite dependent on it. The relationship reaches its final stage; bird and plant are dependent on one another for their survival.

If we contrast the fruit-eating bird with the insectivore, the difference in their way of life is most striking. Insects do not "want" to be eaten. To avoid this, they have evolved all kinds of protective devices; they are cryptically colored and tend to be widely scattered. A bird has usually to spend a great part of its waking day in the search for such food; it will normally eat a vast variety of different insects and so will not be dependent on any one of them.

It is, apparently, the relief from the need to spend most of the day in a search for food that has given the fruit-eaters the opportunity to develop other activities to a degree not seen in the insect-eaters. In a few of the bird families that have entered into close partnership with forest trees as legitimate fruit-eaters there has been an extraordinary proliferation of species with fantastic and beautiful plumages and elaborate courtship displays. In such birds the male's whole life may be centered round a small area—a traditional tree or dancing place on the forest floor. The females come to the display area to mate, after which they carry out all the nesting duties by themselves. In most of these species the males' display areas are more or less closely grouped together in what is known as a "lek." Some leks may be very concentrated, with males occupying display areas or "courts" only a few feet from one another; in others the males may be widely spaced. In the Old World, the birds of paradise are the supreme example of a family that has taken this evolutionary course; in the forests of the New World, the cotingas and manakins, two families closely related to each other but not at all closely related to the birds of paradise, have followed the same path.

I have been lucky enough to have been able to study many

species of cotingas and manakins in the field, in Trinidad and Tobago, the Guianas, Panama, and Brazil. In this book I have picked out some of the most outstanding ones and have tried to describe what they look like and what they do. I have also tried to sketch out some of the wider implications of what might otherwise seem a rather narrow study, in order to show that, while the enjoyment of the beauty of the birds and their surroundings, and the challenge of discovering new facts about their natural history, may be sufficient in themselves to keep one at work in the field for years, the final satisfaction comes from trying to understand why they are as they are.

This is not a book for experts in tropical ornithology, though I hope that any who read it may find a few facts or ideas that will be stimulating. The specialist has his own much more comprehensive and detailed sources of information. The book is intended for anyone who is interested in natural history, or simply curious about the world in general, whether or not his special interest is in birds. Because it is not aimed at the specialist, I have tried to avoid technical terms. The facts and ideas with which natural history is concerned may be put into ordinary language and understood by almost anyone. Two recurring and interrelated themes, however, need some explanation: evolution and adaptation.

There is no doubt that life has evolved and is still evolving, though man has now irrevocably altered the course of future evolution. There is also general agreement among biologists regarding the physical basis of the evolutionary process in sexually reproducing animals such as birds. Each individual has a different genetic constitution, drawn from the total "gene pool" of the species to which it belongs. Those individuals that are by their genetic endowment best fitted to survive themselves and to leave surviving offspring must, on the average, contribute more to the gene pool of succeeding generations than those that are less well endowed. This is the process popularly known as the survival of the fittest; the agency that directs it is natural selection. The result of the process is that the genetic constitution of populations changes gradually, in response to the changing environment. An individual's "fitness" is a composite and complex thing, measurable in theory, embracing all those attributes or characters that may influence its survival or its reproductive success. It is thought by many biologists that there are, in fact, no characters that do not have some influence, and thus that all characters, even those that seem trivial, are subject to natural selection. If correct, this view implies that apparently extravagant structures and adornments, and elaborate courtship displays and other kinds of behavior, are not simply the exuberant expression of some vague evolutionary force, but have evolved under the influence of natural selection and perform some definite function.

Natural selection leads to adaptation. When one says that some character of animal or plant—structural or behavioral—is adapted for some particular function, the word has a precise meaning. One is saying that the character has evolved through natural selection by virtue of its suitability for performing the function in question. Of course one may not *know* that this is so; one can hardly expect to have more than strong indirect evidence for something that happened in the past; but it is sometimes possible to show that the character is *now* performing the function attributed to it. Recent studies in population genetics (in animals other than birds) have shown that natural selection is a very powerful force, and recent studies of the natural history of birds point the same way: whenever some detail of structure of behavior is thoroughly investigated, it is usually found that it has a function, and the inference is that it is "adapted" for this function.

Some of the most successful recent studies of bird behavior have tackled the problem experimentally. This method gives much more convincing results than observation alone. One manipulates the bird's environment, even the bird itself or its nest and eggs, in such a way that a definite answer is obtained —the function of such-and-such a behavior is so-and-so, and this promotes the survival of the individual performing it or the survival of its offspring. The method was used most successfully by Dr. Niko Tinbergen and his colleagues when they wanted to know why Black-headed Gulls remove the hatched eggshells from their nests. They placed eggshells and other objects at various distances from nests, and found that a piece of shell lying near a nest makes the nest more likely to be attacked and destroyed by a Herring Gull or Carrion Crow. Thus a seemingly trivial action, which takes the bird about twenty seconds to perform each year, is of real importance for its breeding success. More often than not, however, one cannot work in this way, and one certainly cannot when observing birds in a tropical forest. So one falls back on collecting as many facts as one can, and by inference, by comparisons between species, and by using what others have found in related fields, one builds up hypotheses that are consistent with biological theory, so far as it is understood.

The desire to explain is deeply rooted and insistent. Without theories and hypotheses one has only a jumble of facts. But one can overindulge in facile explanations; if one's theory is wrong or incomplete one can go badly astray. Certainly our biological theories are very incomplete, for there are so many awkward facts that we cannot begin to account for. Francis Bacon long ago gave a warning that all theorists should heed: "The human understanding is of its own nature prone to suppose the existence of more order and regularity in the world than it finds. And though there be many things which are singular and unmatched, yet it devises for them parallels and conjugates and relations which do not exist." In all that relates to the cotingas and manakins there is much that is singular and unmatched. For this reason I have tried not to overdo the theory. The facts, if accurately observed and described, will stand for all time; the theory can at best be only provisional.

Names

Most of the cotingas and manakins are not very well known yet. There are no English names for them in common use, but instead there are names thought up by ornithologists who, when writing about them, have wanted to give them some English name in addition to their scientific Latin name. These English names are not yet fully standardized, and some of the handbooks use different names from those used here. But the scientific names are more stable, and I list in the Appendix the scientific names of all the species mentioned in the text.

Notes

In order not to distract the general reader, I have kept references out of the text. Instead, a number of key references are given in the Notes at the end of the book (p. 163), numbered according to the place in the text to which they refer. These Notes also deal with odd points of interest which deserve some mention, though they would be out of place or distracting if they were inserted into the main text.

Acknowledgments

My main debt is to my wife. She contributed many of the facts that I give, and a good many of the ideas that I put forward were clarified in discussion with her. A deep debt is also owed to the late David Lack, Director of the Edward Grey Institute of Field Ornithology at Oxford, who arranged for me to go to Trinidad for a few weeks early in 1956 to visit William Beebe's research station in a valley of the forested Northern Range. It would take too much space to list all who have helped me since then, but I cannot omit William Beebe himself, a pioneer in the study of the tropical forest. It was at his invitation that I first went out to Trinidad on this short visit, and his enthusiastic support helped to secure the funds which enabled me to return and work there for four and a half years and make my first trips to the South American mainland.

THE WEB OF ADAPTATION
Bird Studies in the American Tropics

I

The Bellbirds

In the mountains of Central America, northern South America including Trinidad, and eastern Brazil live the four species of bellbirds, each occupying a separate area. For long they have been famous for uttering what are probably the loudest of all bird calls, but otherwise they remained little known, almost mysterious birds, until my wife's study of the Bearded Bellbird in Trinidad made it one of the best known of the cotingas.[1]

I had gone to Trinidad in January 1957, to act as Resident Naturalist at the small tropical research station, until then open for only part of the year, which William Beebe had acquired and presented to the New York Zoological Society. Living surrounded by rich forest in the Arima Valley, in the mountains which run along the north side of Trinidad and represent the last outliers of the eastern Andes, I had been devoting a good deal of my time to birds. I had heard bellbirds often--two or three called not far from the house—but I had hardly had a good view of a calling male and certainly had not considered the idea of a detailed study. The Bearded Bellbird was very much the sort of bird that the visiting birdwatcher just wanted to be able to see—even, perhaps, came to the Arima Valley specially to see—and if he eventually had a glimpse of a white speck on a distant treetop he was satisfied. For another of the peculiarities of the bellbirds is that the males of three of the four species are mainly or entirely white and so at least are conspicuous at a distance if they are exposed to view. Two of them, the White Bellbird of the Guianas and the Bare-throated Bellbird of eastern Brazil, are among the very few land birds with a wholly white plumage.

Barbara came out to Trinidad at the end of May 1958; we were married a day later and had our wedding reception at Spring Hill, high in the Arima Valley, one of the few houses from which bellbirds can regularly be seen. "Difficult" birds are a challenge to her, and she was soon beginning to track down the bellbirds that were calling near St. Pat's, the wooden bungalow where we lived in the lower part of the valley. A bird that seems mysterious and difficult to study may only need rather more than average patience and persistence in the watcher, more willingness to suffer the occasional blank day, and the ability to hold onto and puzzle out the significance of every clue. These qualities Barbara brought to the study of bellbirds, and the account that follows is based almost entirely on her work.

The male Bearded Bellbird is a strangely distinguished looking bird. It has a shortish tail, and is about the size of a Blue Jay but more stockily built. Its body and tail are very pale gray, almost white, the wings black. The head is most striking. The crown and sides of the head are an unusual coffee brown color; the beak is very short and extraordinarily wide at the base; and from the throat hangs a mass of black string-like wattles which gives it its English name.

Bearded Bellbirds live entirely on the fruit of forest trees, which they pluck in flight and swallow whole; hence the very wide gape, which is almost certainly an adaptation enabling them to swallow the largest possible fruits for their size.

Almost all that was known of the habits of the males, when Barbara began her observations, was that they tended to call

Head of male Bearded Bellbird

persistently from the same area of forest; and there were some accounts in the literature, mostly not very accurate, of the way in which the calls are uttered. The call is in fact not very bell-like. The main call is an extraordinarily loud, explosive "bock," which reminds one more of a hammer striking a block of hard wood. This is interspersed with series of less loud notes of essentially the same quality, given at a rate of from one to two and a half notes per second: "tock-tock-tock . . ." The "bock" is easily audible at distances of a mile or more if there is no intervening vegetation.

Once Barbara had tracked down the calling males in the valley near where we lived and had begun to watch them regularly, the situation gradually became clear. There was one calling territory that was apparently most coveted, and near it were two others that were occupied less continuously by males who were always on the lookout for an opportunity to take over the main territory. This favored territory was strategically situated on a slight prominence on a minor ridge some way up a side valley and commanded the approaches from which visiting birds were likely to come.

The bird that occupied this territory called from a number of high, exposed treetops within it, especially early and late in the day and at times when other males were calling nearby; but at other times he came down to much lower perches only fifteen or twenty feet above the ground. These were slender side-branches of small trees of the forest under-story, smooth, slightly drooping, and uncluttered by twigs or leaves. The side-branches of two or three small trees were regularly used, but one was of special importance. It was on the lowest side-branch of this sapling, about fifteen feet above the ground, that the male was visited by females and mating took place.

The male in possession of the favored territory, with its low mating perch, was under constant pressure from rivals, both adult and young males. It was clear that his constant presence and calling were necessary to proclaim his occupation, and this seemed to be the main function of the calling from high perches. Even so, males would often visit him at one of the low perches, as if to check that he was still there, but his presence and aggressive posturing would drive them off. Each year, at the height of his annual molt,[2] he gave up calling for a few weeks and abandoned the territory, and another male would at once take it over; but he regained it at the end of the molt. Late in the study we decided to try to trap this dominant male and color-ring him, so that he could be identified with certainty at his territory or anywhere else. We succeeded in catching him in a net slung across one of his known flight lines, put a ring on his leg and let him go, but the shock was evidently too much for him; he gave up, or was ousted from, his territory at once and a new male took possession, again using the same mating perch.

When a female visits the male at one of the low perches an elaborate ritualized ceremony is enacted, which culminates— if the female is receptive— in mating on the special perch. The early stages of a visit are much the same as when the visitor is a male. The visiting bird first lands on some perch above the low tree in which the male is perched. As soon as the male sees the visitor he falls silent; he then begins a series of ritualized jumps back and forth between his perch and another at about the same level. When he lands after each leap he stays motionless for a few seconds, keeping his eyes fixed on the visitor. His upper breast feathers are puffed out, so that the beard of wattles is pushed prominently forward. If the visitor descends to a lower perch, usually in the upper branches of the display tree, the male moves down to the mating perch, if he is not

The male calling from one of his high perches

already on it. He then begins a sort of stereotyped preening, raising one wing and preening the feathers beneath it, and stretching one leg forward so that a curious patch of deeply colored bare skin is exposed on the thigh. Between preening movements he stares fixedly at the visitor.

Up to this point the owning male's display appears primarily aggressive; at any rate male visitors are usually intimidated by this stage and leave. If the visitor is a female, however, she may not be deterred but may come right down to the mating perch. If she does so, the male's preening movements become less frequent until he is motionless, crouching with his eyes fixed on the female. Usually, he is perched the opposite way on the branch from her, with his head and body turned toward her. Then with a tremendous "bock" he leaps toward the female, turning in the air as he does so. The female may at almost the same moment move away a few feet, in which case the male lands in the place which she has just left. But if she is receptive and stands her ground the male lands on her back and mating follows.

The culmination of courtship: the male about to leap onto the back of the female who has stood her ground

Patience and persistence were essential in getting a clear picture of the behavior of the dominant male and of his visitors and rivals. For instance, Barbara had to continue her observations for three years in order to be sure that the break caused by the molt came at about the same time each year, and in this and other ways to see evidence of the constant pressure from his neighbors of the male in occupation of the central territory. When she began her observations, the male was shy and would leave his mating perch as she approached, but after some weeks she could walk quietly up, sit down within about fifteen yards of him, and begin watching without his even interrupting his calling. She had become a harmless, well-known part of his environment to which he no longer needed to pay special attention.

The picture that gradually emerged was of a group of males competing for a much favored territory, to which the local females came for mating. This constantly occupied territory was the property of the dominant male of the group, always an adult; round it the subordinate adult and nearly adult males occupied, less persistently, their own apparently less satisfactory territories. They were always on the lookout for a chance to take over the best one, but the presence and ritualized threat displays of the owning bird were sufficient to keep them at a distance. In addition a certain number of juvenile males were often about, calling occasionally but not with the full adult voice, and apparently not yet in possession of any proper territory.

A major gap remained: the bellbird's nest and nesting habits, of which almost nothing was known. Until 1954 no nest of any species of bellbird had been found, or at least not by anyone in a position to publish his finding. Then two nests of the Bearded Bellbird were found in Trinidad and were reported to naturalists, one to William Beebe and one to Dr. Wilbur Downs, head of the Trinidad Regional Virus Laboratory. Curiously enough, they were not in the forest but were in cocoa trees in plantations a little distance from the forest edge. They were extremely flimsy stick platforms, built at no great height. One was actually over a footpath. Not much else was found out about these nests, and in fact the reports given to Dr. Beebe by the local people who found the first were almost certainly wrong in two important respects: they referred to the nest having contained two young, and to the male and female being present near the nest.

Female bellbirds are inconspicuous birds. They are uniform olive green above, and dull yellowish white streaked with greenish below. They lack all adornments and are quite silent. In plumage the juvenile males are almost the same, until they begin to acquire some white feathers and to grow their beard, but they are a good deal bigger and much more noisy. The female is only about three-quarters the size of an adult male. It is easy to overlook them entirely, except occasionally when they are feeding at a fruit tree or, of course, if one happens to be watching a male at his display tree.

It was in October 1958 that Barbara saw a female bellbird pick a slender twig from a small tree and fly off with it. The tree was on the forest edge, beside the road which passed the bottom of our garden and continued up the valley, and only a little way from the house. The bird flew across the narrow valley toward some Indian houses about 150 yards away and went into a tree quite near one of the houses.

From then on Barbara did not look back. This female, or perhaps this bird and another, built a succession of nests over the next three years, all within an area of about an acre, in the trees that grew around one of the Indian houses, whose owner was the caretaker of the estate on which our house stood.

Though strictly a forest bird, it is probably quite usual for female bellbirds to seek a nest site outside the forest itself, as our bird did and the two birds whose nests had been found earlier had done. Because of the abundance of nest predators, especially snakes, a very high proportion of all nests in tropical forests fail. Isolated trees in a clearing outside the forest are almost certainly safer. In the natural state, Trinidad bellbirds probably chose clearings caused by tree falls, or the open leads of stream courses. Today the cultivated land adjoining the forest, planted with mango, cocoa, and other useful trees, forms an ideal nesting habitat.

Nobody is likely to find a bellbird's nest by looking for the nest itself. It is, for the size of the bird, an extraordinarily small and flimsy-looking pad of twigs, hardly more conspicuous than any small cluster of twigs in the branches in which it is placed. But it is much stronger than it looks. Each of the Arima Valley nests was built of the same materials. The main part of the pad was made almost entirely of terminal twigs of a large forest tree, the "white olivier" (*Terminalia obovata*), which are typically forked and slightly curved and have characteristic knobby or club-shaped endings where the leaf scars are. The shallow nest cup, only two inches across, was made solely of forked terminal twigs of a small tree with unusually small leaves locally known at "ti-fay," a corruption of the French patois name "petit-feuille" (*Maprounea guianensis*). This tree has very fine twigs, springy and curved, with close-set thickenings or nodes for the leaf attachments. The nodes catch on one another when several twigs are forced together, even more effectively than the clubbed endings of the white olivier twigs. Even so, it was remarkable how the bellbird's simple nest-building movements formed a rather small number of these two sorts of twigs into a structure compact and strong enough to hold the egg, the incubating female, and then the growing nestling for two months, through rain that was sometimes torrential and wind that tossed the branches among which it was placed.

There is no doubt that the keynote of the bellbird's nesting

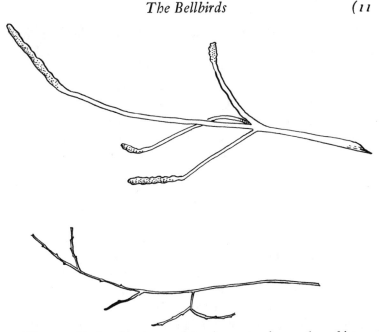

The two kinds of twigs used in the nest: above, the white olivier (*Terminalia obovata*); below, ti-fay (*Maprounea guianensis*)

strategy is inconspicuousness. First and foremost, only the cryptically colored female ever goes near the nest; the conspicuous males, intent on attracting females to their display perches and on keeping rival males away, have nothing to do with the nest. Then, not only is the nest itself as inconspicuous as it could be; the whole behavior of the nesting female, and even of the nestling, seems designed to draw as little attention as possible to themselves and to the position of the nest. It is only while she is building that the female's visits to the nest are frequent enough to give an observer, or a potential predator, much chance of locating the nest by watching her; and even then, because of the relatively small number of twigs in the completed nest, her visits must be much fewer than those made by birds of most other species when they are bulding. After the single egg is laid—a well camouflaged egg, light tan in ground color and mottled with brown—she incubates in long spells.

We watched at one nest continuously for a whole day and found that the female left the nest only five times, each absence averaging about twenty minutes. Her last absence ended at 4:18 P.M., after which she remained on the nest for the remainder of the afternoon and on through the night. Later as incubation progressed, her last absence of the day ended earlier and earlier, until she was sitting continuously from 2 P.M. and on through the night. When the chick hatches, after twenty-three days of incubation, the female's visits to the nest become more frequent, but even then the visits are only approximately hourly, much less frequent than the feeding visits of most other songbirds. During one complete day's watch a chick received only eleven feeds. The chick is reared entirely on fruit, mostly of kinds that the adults themselves eat. The female feeds it by regurgitation and it takes her little time to collect enough to fill the stomach of her chick as well as to satisfy her own needs.

On hatching, the chick is already covered with a thick whitish down, and this apparently enables it to be left, curled up on the tiny nest and looking rather like a large hairy white caterpillar, at a much earlier age than most nestlings are left unexposed. We hardly saw the female brood her chick at all after it was three or four days old; she simply flew in, fed it, and swooped away out of the tree after a minute or two. Evidently it is safer for the female to leave the nest and chick, except for brief visits with food, as soon as the chick can maintain its body temperature adequately. Probably the reason is that the nest with the female sitting on it or near it is more conspicuous than when she is not there. Discovery is what must be avoided at all costs.

Everything that happens at the nest is silent, and movement is reduced to a minimum. The chick lies motionless for most of the time. It begs for food by merely raising its head and gaping, with none of the high-pitched begging calls that are so characteristic of most nestlings. When the female comes to feed it she flies swiftly and silently in, lands on a perch near the nest, remains motionless for a minute or so, evidently, checking that no danger threatens, then hops to the nest. Once, when the female came to one of the nests which we were watching, she found us too close for her liking. We had put a ladder up to the nest, and I was climbing it to inspect the small nestling. Unlike most other birds, which would have shown alarm, calling and moving about and perhaps trying to distract us, she simply remained absolutely motionless and silent where she had landed, a few feet from the nest, and finally flew swiftly and silently off.

In spite of all these precautions nesting success is probably not very high. Of the five nests in which we knew that eggs had been laid, only one was successful. Wind destroyed one nest, which was badly sited near the end of a horizontal branch, and three nests lost their eggs, probably to predators, during incubation. The successful nestling flew at an age of thirty-three days. When it was about half-grown we had put a red ring on one leg, on the off-chance that we might be able to follow its later progress. It did not seem at all likely that we would, as young birds suffer a high mortality and they also wander.

For over a year we saw nothing of it, and we gave up hope of ever seeing it again. Then in November 1960, sixteen months after it had left the nest, we suddenly saw it again in the forest near the house, and from then on we saw it almost weekly until it was two years old. Luckily, he was a male. When we first saw him he was still in juvenile plumage, but small buds of wattles were beginning to appear on his throat. Three months later the first white feathers were beginning to grow, and when we saw the last of him, at an age of just over two years, he was about halfway from the green juvenile plumage to the white, black, and coffee color of the adult, and his beard of wattles was still short. All this time he had been practicing his calls. He had already got past the stage of making uncoordinated squawks and squeaks which are all that the males can produce when they first start to call. His "bock" was more staccato than the adult's and its timing was variable; his repeated "tocks" were very juvenile and husky. Five months later his "bock" seemed to be perfected, but the "tock" was still husky and remained so until he was last seen.

This lucky chance told us some important things about the development of young bellbirds. In particular it showed us

Head of male Bare-throated Bellbird

that males may take a long time to reach adulthood, that the calls, although simple, need a prolonged period of learning, and that the part of the repertoire that needs most coordination, the repeated "tock-tock-tock . . . ," takes longer to learn than the simpler "bock." We could never hope again to slip a color ring on a nestling's leg and gain so much from it.

The three other species of bellbirds are much less well known. No nest has been reported of any of them, not even the Bare-throated Bellbird which is found in the wooded mountains close to the city of Rio de Janeiro and is regularly caught and exported to European and American zoos. It is fairly certain that the behavior of all of them is basically similar to that of the Bearded Bellbird; the most striking differences are in the plumage and ornamentation of the males, and in their calls.

I have watched the Bare-throated Bellbird, not very successfully, in the forested mountains of the state of São Paulo in southeastern Brazil. Without doubt it is very closely related to the Bearded Bellbird. Although the plumage of the male Bare-throated Bellbird is entirely white, it agrees closely with the Bearded in other characteristics: both have a bare throat, green-skinned in the Bare-throated, wattled in the Bearded; in both the outer flight feathers are curiously modified in the same way; both have a bare patch on the side of the thigh which is exposed in display. Both too utter the same tremendous "bock," like a hammer striking a cracked anvil; but the Bare-throated Bellbird's repeated note, corresponding to the repeated "tock" of the Bearded, ends in a very sharp ringing sound exactly an octave above the pitch of the first part of the note, as if the hammer had struck the anvil a glancing blow and caused it to ring.

On two expeditions to Guyana we have watched the White Bellbird in the forests of the Kanuku Mountains in the south of the country, near the Brazilian border. This is *the* bellbird, the only one whose voice is really bell-like and the one which stirred the imagination of the early travelers in the Guianas. The male is snowy white, with a curious single black wattle, studded with small white feathers, growing from the base of the upper mandible.

Charles Waterton heard it once in his *Wanderings in South America*, and tried but failed to shoot it. He started the error which subsequent writers all repeated, that the wattle can be inflated with air by the bird at will and then sticks up like a spire from its forehead. To make up for this, he wrote eloquently of the mysterious bird in its forest setting, giving it its Spanish name "campanero." "With many of the feathered race, he pays the common tribute of a morning and an evening song; and even when the meridian sun has shut in silence the mouths of almost the whole of animated nature, the campanero still cheers the forest. You hear his toll, and then a pause for a minute, then another toll, and then a pause again, and then a toll, and again a pause. Then he is silent for six or eight minutes, and then another toll, and so on. Acteon would stop in mid chase, Maria would defer her evening song, and Orpheus himself would drop his lute to listen to him, so sweet, so novel, and romantic is the toll of the pretty snow-white campanero. He is never seen to feed with the other cotingas, nor is it known in what part of Guiana he makes his nest."

For more than a hundred years, inspired by Waterton, naturalists visiting the Guianas had high among their aims the desire to see the White Bellbird; but they never found out much about it because they at once tried to shoot the bird as soon as they had found it. Richard Schomburgk, who

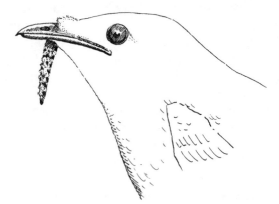

Head of male White Bellbird

traveled in the Kanuku Mountains in the 1840s, added greatly to our knowledge of the country, its plants, and its animals, but he made no progress with the bellbird. "So we went on for about an hour," he wrote of the only occasion when he saw one, "and my strength was beginning to fail—when suddenly there sounded not far from us the magical chime of the bellbird, the goal of my desires; and soon the sharp eyes of the Indians had picked out the singer on the top of an old, dead Mora tree. After much effort I too managed to see the white bird in the blinding sunlight." His account then degenerates. He at once tried to shoot the bird, and finally succeeded, and he goes on to describe, in words very similar to Waterton's, how the wattle is inflated with air and sticks up like a horn.

Although the wattle always hangs limply, it is in fact extensible. When the bird is not calling, the wattle shrinks up to a short fat worm, so that it does not impede the bird as it feeds; when the bird begins to call, it lengthens out to several inches and hangs down well below the level of the head. The change is probably brought about by longitudinal muscle fibers, since the alteration in shape can be rapid. The throat wattles of the Bearded Bellbird are similarly extensible, but far less strikingly so.

The White Bellbird has two calls: a very loud double note, "kong-kay," like two sharp blows on a very slightly cracked bell, and a long drawn-out chime of pure quality, "do-i-i-i-ing," usually followed a fraction of a second later by a fainter echo. It is this silvery chime, filtering down through the forest trees from an unseen caller, that must have most stirred the imagination of travelers in the remote hill country to which the White Bellbird is confined.

The double "kong-kay" is a remarkable call for another reason. There are two renderings. Sometimes it is uttered with the head held still, but a louder version of it is given with a violent swing of the head and body. The swing is always from right to left. The bird turns slightly to the right for the "kong, and then an instant later swings the head sharply to the left uttering the "kay" as it does so. As the head swings, the wattle streams out behind. The swing is always the same way, and the wattle must be lying at the right-hand side of the beak beforehand, otherwise it would simply get in the way and enter the widely open mouth. Occasionally the wattle gets to the wrong side, and when this happens the bird maneuvers it back to the right side before attempting the "kong-kay." On our first visit to the Kanuku Mountains, Barbara was able to watch only one male, and so could not be certain that this was not merely an individual habit. On our long visit in 1970 we watched several birds, and all were "right-wattled." Later, searching for early references to cotingas in *Timehri*, the excellent journal published for many years by the Georgetown Museum, I came across the following account by J. J. Quelch of the calling behavior of a White Bellbird that lived in captivity for a short time in Georgetown, in 1890; it too was evidently right-wattled, so there seems no doubt that it is a specific character of all White Bellbirds.

When the appendage is fully elongated [he has earlier described the lengthening and shortening of the wattle], the bird suddenly inflates its lungs, right and left, by inhaling—almost by a swallowing action—two great draughts of air; but the method by which this is done depends upon which of its two characteristic notes it intends to utter. When the notes "Kong-kay" are uttered, the action of inflation has been performed by two distinct inhalations of air, one with the head turned to the right and the other immediately after to the left. At the moment of utterance of the notes, the head is turned to the right for the "Kong," and then suddenly—so suddenly that it almost startles the observer—the head is swung round to the left for the "Kay," which is issued with a strikingly loud, piercing and metallic ring or clang—so loud indeed that, if the observer is close by, the ears are actually deafened for the moment by the sharpness of the sound.

When, however, the sweet, musical, and deeply-toned bell-like notes "Do-rong" [what I have called the "do-i-i-i-ing"] are about to be uttered, the bird is observed simply to hold its head forward, and to make two distinct gulps of air; and then, holding its beak upwards and slightly extending its neck, the notes are rolled out, as it were, with full voice and roundness and resonance.

Quelch's account strongly suggests that the two notes are made by air expelled separately from the two lungs; in which case it would seem likely that one note is made by the vibration of one of the paired membranes in the syrinx, and the other note by vibration of the membrane on the other side. This might also be the explanation of the unusual ringing sound of the repeated call of the Bare-throated Bellbird, caused by a note one octave higher than, and overlapping in time with, the main hammerlike note. Some songbirds are known to be able to utter two, or even three, notes simultaneously, and it seems certain that two or more membranes in the syrinx must vibrate independently; but there is no known case of the successive expulsion of air from the two lungs to produce two notes.[3]

To end with the Three-wattled Bellbird is an anticlimax. It is not well known, and is the only one of the four that I cannot write about from personal knowledge. And anything I say will soon be superseded, for as I write Barbara is watching it in the mountains of western Costa Rica. Nothing has been reported of its courtship, and the few published accounts of its voice are conflicting. One can at least say that it is peculiar in a number of ways. It differs most strikingly from the other bellbirds in the chestnut brown body plumage of the male,

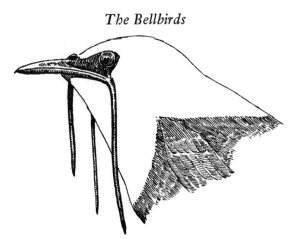

Head of male Three-wattled Bellbird

clearly demarcated from the white head and neck. It breeds
—or almost certainly does, for no nest has been found—in the
high montane forests of Central America, from southern Hon-
duras to western Panama. From about March to July, the
period when most other birds are nesting, the males call constantly in these high forests; they then move down to the
lowlands, right down to sea level and even to some of the
islands that lie off the coast of Panama, in the longest vertical
migration known for any Central American bird.

Little is known of their behavior, except for the calls
which have been described by Alexander Skutch.[4] There are
two different notes: one "loud and strong but dull and
throaty, such as might be produced by striking once a
wooden bell devoid of resonance," the other much sharper
and higher in pitch. Typically the first note is followed by
the second, but they may be delivered in almost any combination. They are never, it seems, uttered in very long series,
and even in a short series the notes become increasingly faint.

It is tempting to speculate on the origin of the Three-
wattled Bellbird and the reason why its voice is, as it
seems, so different from the voices of the three other species.
Without much doubt it is most closely related to the White
Bellbird. Just as the Bearded and Bare-throated Bellbirds resemble one another in several characters, so do the White and
Three-wattled Bellbirds. Both have a feathered throat, and a

wattle or wattles growing from the base of the beak. Both have fully feathered thighs, and their outer flight feathers are modified in the same way. The Three-wattled Bellbird is probably an offshoot from the ancestral stock of the White Bellbird, which at some time in the past—perhaps not very long ago—established itself by the long-range dispersal of a group of pioneering individuals, under what climatic or environmental circumstances we shall never know. It is usually young birds that actively disperse and settle in new areas, and so it may well have happened that the population of bellbirds newly established in Central America, from which the three-wattled species has descended, was founded by birds with unformed repertoires. Our record of the young Bearded Bellbird which was ringed in the nest showed that at least two years of learning may be needed before the fully adult calls are mastered; and the presence of calling adults is almost certainly a necessary condition for learning the normal calls of the species. It might be expected, therefore, that when the vocabulary of the newly established Central American bellbird population stabilized it would have become very different from that of the parental population.

Something of the same sort may also have happened to the Trinidad population of Bearded Bellbirds. When we were thoroughly familiar with the calls of the Trinidad birds, we heard Paul Schwartz's beautiful gramophone record[5] of Venezuelan bird songs and were surprised to hear that Venezuelan Bearded Bellbirds have three different calls, the explosive "bock" and the repeated "tocks," which we knew, and a double, repeated "kering-kerong, kering-kerong. . . ," more musical than the two other calls, in fact almost bell-like. This must be the call that gives the Bearded Bellbird in Venezuela the first part of its local name, *Campanero herrero*, the bellman blacksmith. Until then we had been puzzled by the earliest detailed description of the calls of the Trinidad bellbird. In 1893 two very distinguished American ornithologists, William Brewster and Frank M. Chapman, visited Trinidad briefly, and among other things described the calls of the Bearded Bellbird in the Montserrat Hills in the center of the island. They described three different calls, two of which were clearly the "bock" and the repeated "tock." The third was so different from anything we had heard that we wondered whether they had made a mistake, unlikely though this seemed. It was "a 'tui' closely followed by a metallic 'ting' which sounds exactly like an echo and appears to be of almost the same duration and nearly as loud as the 'tui.'" Allowing for the fact that Brewster and Chapman's verbalizing of the "tock," which they wrote as "tang," suggests a purer and higher-pitched note than seems right to us, this is a very good description of the "kering-kerong." Thus there seems little doubt that the bellbirds of central Trinidad had the full repertoire of the Venezuelan population in 1893. Whether the bellbirds of the Northern Range also did so will never be known. The Montserrat Hills are now mainly deforested and there are no bellbirds left there. Probably at some time in the past the bellbirds of the Northern Range were much reduced in numbers so that there were not enough adult males to pass on the tradition. It may be significant that the element which has been lost is the most complex, and thus the one which would be expected to take the longest to learn.

2

The Cock-of-the-Rock

In the interior of the three Guianas and adjacent parts of northern Brazil, extending west into southern Venezuela, is a great tract of mountainous country, the Guiana highlands. The mountains are mostly not very high, and they do not form a continuous range. In the eastern half of the area the Kanukus and other ranges rise to 3–4,000 feet; in the west the famous table-topped mountains of Venezuela, with sheer walls, rise to 8–9,000 feet. Mount Roraima, one of the highest, at the point where Guyana, Brazil, and Venezuela meet, was the setting for Conan Doyle's novel, *The Lost World*, and was the childhood home of Rima, the heroine of W. H. Hudson's novel *Green Mansions*.

The Guiana highlands are the remnant of a very ancient block of elevated land, now mostly eroded. Though the primitive creatures which Conan Doyle imagined do not survive there, the highlands have nevertheless been a minor evolutionary center for South American birds. Two of the species which almost certainly evolved in the area, and are still largely confined to it, rank high among the most interesting and beautiful birds of the continent. One, the White Bellbird, I have already described; the other is the Cock-of-the-rock.

Skins of the Cock-of-the-rock were known to Linnaeus, and at least enough of its habits to enable him to give it the appropriate name *Rupicola*, the dweller among rocks. It is about the size of a small crow, stockily built with strong legs and a somewhat hooked beak. But the plumage of the male is so brilliant and extravagantly modified as to quite transform it; looking at it, one has the impression not so much of a bird as of some confection of golden orange feathers, set off with a little black and white and edged with silky filaments of gold. The head is surmounted by a double crest of orange feathers, meeting along the midline to form an almost perfect semi-circle when seen from the side, and coming down over the beak in front so as to hide it almost completely. The semi-circular outline of the crest is subtly emphasized by a fine line of deep purple inset a little from the margin. The body is entirely golden orange, and the feathers of the lower back are fan-shaped, broadened and angular at the tips, and form a sort of shield which almost hides the short tail. More remark-able still are the innermost flight feathers, which are modified to an altogether more extreme degree. Not only are they broad and angular at the tip, but the fringes of the outer vanes are prolonged into silky filaments that project at each side of the body and are so light that they move in the slightest breeze. The wing, lying below and largely concealed by this silky fringe, is black with a white speculum, conspicuous in flight but not very noticeable at rest. The orange color per-vades the whole body as well as most of the plumage, for the eye is bright orange red, the beak and legs are orange yellow, and even the skin is orange.

The female is a very different bird, drab brown with only a hint of the male's finery in the shape of a small coxcomb on the crown, a stunted version of the male's magnificent crest, which merely gives the head a faintly ludicrous appearance. Her lack of any other adornment reveals a rather heavy, un-gainly form, but she is nevertheless surprisingly agile in flight.

In the late eighteenth and nineteenth centuries skins of the adult males were naturally much prized by "cabinet naturalists," and the Cock-of-the-rock became famous. As so often happens, the little that was known, or thought to be known, about the bird was a mixture of truth, half-truth, and outright error. It was known to be associated with rocks, but was thought to be a ground-living bird, a sort of game bird, and was often pictured perched on a rock on some mountainside.[6] In fact, the association with rocks is more specific: the nest is a bracket of mud, fixed to a vertical rock face; the birds themselves are forest-dwelling fruit-eaters, like the other large cotingas. It was known that the males gather at dancing grounds—indeed it was by trapping them at their dancing grounds that the Indians were able to obtain the skins which found their way to Europe—but the early accounts of the dancing grounds were most misleading. They suggested that a group of males gathered at the chosen place, and that each in turn performed some sort of dance while the others looked on. The function of the dance remained a matter for speculation. As usual, the trouble was that the birds were too highly prized as specimens. Few people, having reached the habitat of the Cock-of-the-rock and been guided by local Indians to a dancing ground, were willing to watch for long before the coveted specimens were collected and the birds scattered. And in a few minutes, especially if no hide has been built in advance, one can see little of what goes on at a Cock-of-the-rock dancing ground. An account published in 1910 by a zoo collector, W. Frost,[7] gave what appeared to be a more accurate picture of the organization of a dancing ground. Frost's description suggested that the males did not each display in turn on a common dance floor, but that each owned and displayed on its own small court within the general display area, as the males of other lek birds do.

In 1960 Barbara and I visited the Kanuku Mountains for a week, on what could be little more than a reconnaissance. We camped with Jim Fowler, an American falconer who for some months had been carrying out a remarkable study of the Harpy Eagle, the huge monkey-eating eagle of tropical America. Scaling with ropes an immense silk-cotton tree in which a pair of eagles was nesting, he had trapped an adult and a young bird and was training them in the camp. We spent a few days watching the manakins and other cotingas which we had come to study, and the Cock-of-the-rock hardly entered our thoughts. But when Jim Fowler told us that he had visited a dancing ground about ten miles away and offered to take us there in his battered jeep, we decided that the chance was too good to be missed and we devoted our last two days to the expedition.

It must have been the most accessible Cock-of-the-rock dancing ground in the whole mountain range. All the others that we subsequently heard of or visited were a good deal more remote. We left the forest, and bumped for several miles along rough tracks through the open savanna on which the forested hills abruptly abut. Then we left the jeep and took a small, overgrown path which wound up into the forest, crossing one or two gullies, until after climbing perhaps three hundred feet it led into an area of more open forest, with little undergrowth, on a ridge. As we approached, we heard the uncouth crowing squawks of the disturbed male birds, and got a few glimpses of the brilliant orange apparitions as they vanished among the trees. On the ground were the unmistakable signs that we were at the right place: about half a dozen cleared patches on the forest floor, each two or three feet across and spaced several yards apart. All the fallen dead leaves had been cleared from these courts, and the bark had been stripped from the exposed rootlets.

Before he left to return to his eagles, Jim Fowler took us to a jumble of boulders the size of houses, about two hundred yards further up the hillside, attached to which were the mud brackets of three nests, all unluckily empty. Our plan was to conceal ourselves and watch at the dancing ground for the remaining hours of daylight, then sling our hammocks for the night between trees nearby, watch again the next morning, and at about midday begin to walk back to camp. We had a tin or two of sardines and some matches, but little else. We knew which direction we had come across the savanna, skirting the forest edge, and judged that by walking back the same way we would be bound eventually to find the dirt track which entered the forest and led to the camp.

It was a rather disappointing attempt. We could not conceal ourselves well enough in the very limited time available. The males came back into the trees above their courts; they were suspicious, continually making little bobbing movements and snapping their beaks, and they would not come down low. We then passed a very exposed night, hoping that no jaguar would come sniffing round our hammocks. Next morning the birds were no more reassured. No doubt this dancing ground had been visited too often by Indians, and the birds had reason to be timid. Accordingly, at midday we picked our way out of the forest and began the hottest and thirstiest walk we can remember. Our water soon gave out. Long tongues of forest, with thick undergrowth, reached out into the savanna, and we either had to outflank them or had to plough through them, without knowing which was the more feasible. We never found the previous day's jeep track.

Eventually, after covering a distance which we thought should have brought us near to the camp, we came upon an Indian house on an open knoll. The woman gave us as much dirty water to drink as we needed, and although we did not speak each other's language we managed to persuade the husband to guide us back to the camp, which he knew about. He at once set off at a great pace, which we soon realized was very necessary as we had many miles still to go, along tracks which we would never have been able to follow without his guidance. We reached camp well after dark and drank numerous mugs of tea and cocoa.

The following September I visited the American Museum of Natural History in New York. The late Dr. Tom Gilliard, an authority on the birds of paradise, was on the staff, and I told him of our visit to the Cock-of-the-rock dancing ground, and how relatively easily accessible it was. He was, as it happened, keen to compare the birds of paradise, whose display grounds he had visited in New Guinea, with what seemed to be their nearest counterpart in the New World, and he went off to Guyana early in the following year. I did not know that, and when I returned to the Kanuku Mountains in March 1961, with a few days available in which to try to see something more of the Cock-of-the-rock, I found that Tom had just left after camping for three weeks near the dancing ground, and had left behind not only a palm-thatched shelter but also a well-built hide of palm thatch in a strategic spot at the dancing ground. The birds had become used to it, and in the four days that I was there I saw the males' strange performance.[8]

Each of the adult males at a dancing ground holds its own court on the forest floor, and spends much of the day in the trees near the court, on low perches immediately beside it, or on the court itself. In the trees above, the males tend to be aggressive to each other and are especially aggressive to intruding males. When no female is present they spend much time in a group, often out to one side of the main area of the courts; they do a great deal of jockeying for position among themselves, squawking and displacing each other from their perches, and occasionally briefly fighting. While doing so they adopt characteristic poses and make stereotyped movements; frequently they cling sideways to vertical saplings with the tail tucked well in under the body, sometimes with the wings half spread. When they are on horizontal perches they constantly make little bobbing bows forward, with a click of the beak as they sharply raise their head at the end of the bow. Occasionally there is a short chase. The general picture is one of slight confusion and apparently aimless bursts of excitement, punctuated at intervals by crowing squawks.

Occasionally the scene is transformed. The birds swiftly move down to their courts, landing with a single squawk and a momentary fanning of their wings, which reveals the white patch on the black flight feathers and not only makes the landing bird additionally conspicuous but serves to blow away any dead leaves or other light debris that may be lying on the court. After landing, the males crouch motionless on the bare earth, like so many fallen flowers of brilliant orange. The body is held horizontally and somewhat flattened, the legs are flexed, and the head is turned sideways so that the crest is in the horizontal plane and one eye is looking upward. The only movement may be the slight stirring of the silky fringes of the wing feathers projecting beyond the sides of the body. The position may be held for several minutes with only the slightest movements, such as a slow turning of the head or a slight hitch or turn of the body. Sometimes a more vigorous movement is made: the bird bobs its head downward, with a click of the beak as it raises it again, or jumps into the air with a squawk and conspicuously fanning wings, to land back in the crouching posture again.

The stimulus for the sudden descent to the courts, and for the change from noisy aggressiveness to statuesque posturing, is the arrival of a female or females at the dancing ground. For a watcher in a hide, with only a small slit or window to watch through, it is often impossible to know whether or not a female is present in the trees above. All that I can say from my own experience is that the males came down to their courts whenever I knew or strongly suspected that a female was present. At other times there may have been no female present and the males may have been displaying as it were *in vacuo*, as manakins also often do in the absence of a female.

In my four days of observation in 1961 I saw no female come down to a court. They were clearly interested but remained ten feet or more up in the trees. In the previous three weeks Tom Gilliard saw, once, what he interpreted as the choice of a male by a visiting female. "The high point of my observations," he wrote, "came one afternoon when I saw a female choose her mate. Eight feet up and 20 feet away, she perched for about five minutes while she surveyed the three brilliant males contorting themselves before her. Suddenly, without warning, she dived toward the ground, aiming at the male in the center. She struck the earth a few inches from him, hitting it so hard that I heard the sound distinctly from 25 feet away. There was an immediate loud squawk, probably from the male, who then flew in pursuit. The female had not paused for even a moment, but rebounded like a skipped stone. They flew out of sight together and presumably mated."

I could not accept this interpretation of the incident. Indeed, Gilliard himself remarked that he would have been more confident of his interpretation if he had not on another occasion seen rather similar chases when a band of what were probably young males persistently pestered the adult males at their courts. All our experience of other lek birds—manakins, cotingas, and hummingbirds—as well as the experience of others who had studied such lek species as Ruffs and Black Grouse, showed that mating takes place at the lek, on the court or display perch, after some form of ritualized display. Half the point of the male Cock-of-the-rock's elaborate courtship posturing and brilliance seemed to be lost if the female's visit ended in a chase away from the dancing ground and the court which should have been the center of her interest. I felt sure that something more must happen at the dancing grounds, to which the displays we had seen were merely the preliminaries.

Nine years later, in 1970, we went back to the Kanukus, Barbara for her second and I for my third visit. This time we were to be there for nearly three months and the cotingas were the main object of our visit. Jan Lindblad, the Swedish wildlife photographer, had been there the year before and had told us that his last camp might be an ideal base for our operations. We decided to go there first, and if necessary move elsewhere for the second half of our stay. In the event we stayed there for the whole of the eleven weeks. It did indeed prove to be an ideal base; nearly all the species we hoped to find were to be found within walking distance. Our experience retaught us a lesson that we had learnt before but I am always in danger of forgetting: if you want to study a new species of bird in the field and have found a place where it occurs, don't start moving about hoping to find a better place; keep at it when you have found the birds, even if results seem to come slowly; for every day adds to your knowledge and understanding by compound interest; each new fact becomes more significant in the light of what is already known.

Jan Lindblad's old camp was situated on a small area of level ground beside one of the small rivers that flow down from the Kanuku Mountains. It was only a short distance inside the forest and was beside a trail which led to a small Indian "garden," or patch of cultivation, a mile and a half up the valley and then on, as a hunting trail, for several more miles. A family of Macusi Indians, who lived on the open savanna some miles away, cultivated the garden and occasionally spent a night or two here in a rough shelter. Otherwise the country upstream from the camp was entirely uninhabited; we were on the edge of a great tract of rough mountainous country, forest-covered except for some of the steepest peaks and jutting rocky bluffs, and undisturbed except for a few Indians hunting with bows and arrows. There were birds in great variety, including the larger species which cannot stand much contact with modern man, and mammals were unusually abundant and tame.

One of the attractions of the camp site was that there was a nesting place of the Cock-of-the-rock only a little way up the hillside immediately above it. There was also a dancing ground two hours' walk up the valley. I decided to devote some of my time in the following weeks to a third and more thorough attempt to find out more about the behavior of the Cock-of-the-rock, and in particular to see the culminating stages of the courtship.[9] At the same time, with any luck, I should have an opportunity to add to the very little that was known of the bird's nesting habits.

William, the Macusi Indian who looked after our camp, had worked for Jan Lindblad and knew the dancing ground. He guided me to it for my first visit and I chose a place that seemed suitable for a hide. Jan had built two the previous year but hardly a vestige remained of them. The dancing ground was at a much greater height than the one I had visited ten years earlier, probably about 1,000 feet up the hillside from the riverbed. It was on a steep, tangled forest ridge, strewn with large boulders, so that it was impossible to find a place from which more than two or three of the ten cleared courts could be seen. I selected a spot about twenty feet from two courts which appeared to be in active use. Jan Lindblad had had one of his hides in the same place and on one occasion, I was told, had found it occupied by a bushmaster; but it seemed so much the best place that I thought it worth risking the return of the snake. William went back a fews days later by himself and built a hide, cutting and lashing together saplings for a framework and thatching the sides and top with palm fronds, a useful material for hides which is never in short supply in the Kanukus. He returned, shaken, saying that a fer-de-lance had struck at him soon after he left the dancing ground, but had only hit his trousers.[10] I never found a bush-

master in my hide and we had no further incidents with
snakes, but they were more abundant, or at least more often
seen, than in any other forest we had been in. On most days
one or both of us saw a snake of some kind, the largest of
which was a boa constrictor about ten feet long. The largest
snake of all, the anaconda, had been found by Jan Lindblad in
the stream not far from the camp, but we never saw one.

I had several sessions in the hide, and at the same time I made
regular checks on the nests near the camp, and on two other
more distant nest sites which William showed me. The breeding season had not yet started, but last year's nests were being
repaired. Fresh mud was being added to the nests, and the
rocks below were spattered with blobs of mud and regurgitated seeds. Sometimes I flushed a female from a nest as I
approached. It seemed likely that egg laying would soon
start. The females were presumably visiting the dancing
grounds, and mating was probably taking place or about to do
so. For a considerable part of four days I sat in the hide and
saw the same activity as I had seen nine years before. The
males were constantly present; they would come down to
their courts and crouch motionless, occasionally giving a little
hitch or a bob, or jump up with a squawk and a flutter of the
wings. Sometimes I could see that a female was present overhead, sometimes I heard one; but I only once saw one come
down to a court.

This was about midday on March 4. There was an obvious
increase in excitement among the males, and the two males
whose courts were in view dropped down onto them at the
same moment, and crouched. Shortly afterwards a female
landed on the nearer of the two courts. She alighted behind the crouching male, hopped up to him, and then, leaning
forward, began to nibble at the long silky fringes of his modified wing feathers. She was nervous, apparently of the hide,
and moved away a couple of feet after about ten seconds;
then she approached him again, and again began to nibble at
the golden fringe of the motionless male.

I was in a tantalizing position. Just before this happened,
having spent about three hours in the cramped hide and seen
no female come down, I had decided to leave, but thought

that I would first try for some photographs of the males at their courts, and so had stuck the telephoto lens of my camera out of the small hole through which I watched. Now I did not dare to move the camera, nor to take a photograph, as the movement or the click of the shutter might well alarm the female; and holding the camera still was becoming a strain. Finally, while the female was nibbling the male's feathers for the second time, I decided to take one picture and slowly withdraw the camera. I could have cursed the Exacta's loud shutter; it alarmed the female and she flew off—and the photograph later turned out to be hopelessly underexposed. She remained nearby, calling occasionally, and the males remained frozen on their courts for several minutes; but she did not come down again. There was then a general scare and all the birds flew off.

While the female was down on the court, a curious whining squawking went on continuously in the trees overhead, and contrasting with the silence of the statically displaying males gave an impression of intense excitement to the whole scene. Later, when the female had flown up from the court and was calling nearby, with the usual monosyllabic crowing squawk, another bird was calling in the same way from the other end of the dancing ground. It seemed probable that two females had visited the dancing ground together, one of which had uttered the whining sound while watching the other's approaches to the male on his court.

Almost certainly, this remarkable behavior of the female, which I had been lucky enough to see, is the immediate prelude to mating. If what I saw was typical—and it probably was, since for obvious reasons one is always much more likely to see the usual rather than the unusual—it explains the extravagant development of the fringes of the male's wing feathers: they play a direct part in the sequence of mating behavior and are presumably sexually stimulating to the female.

I never saw a female come down to a male's court again. Gilliard saw only the one incident quoted above, which in fact probably involved a young male, although he watched for about three weeks. His visit was a little earlier in the year than mine, and the females may not have been quite ready to lay; but even if this was so, it still seems that the male Cock-of-the-rock receives fewer visits at his court than the males of other lek species which have been watched.

On our first visit to the Kanukus the three nests which we examined were empty. This was a disappointment as little was known of the Cock-of-the-rock's nesting habits. On my second visit, when I camped for four days near the same dancing ground, an egg was laid in one of the nests while I was there, at the extreme end of March. An early report had mentioned eggs being found in March, and the Indians traditionally visit the nesting places to take young birds in May. Thus we had good reason to expect egg laying during our long visit in 1970, which lasted from mid-January to early April.

The three old nests on the hillside above our camp were attached to vertical rock faces in a cleft deep inside a shattered mass of huge rocks. One nest was twelve feet up and I had to inspect it with a mirror attached to a long pole; one was low down and could be looked into without difficulty; and the third overhung a deep fissure and was inaccessible except by ropes from above, but it could be looked into from a vantage point about fifteen feet away and a little above it. I inspected these three nests every other day, and either William or I visited the two more distant nest sites regularly. The females began to repair their old nests in early February. I found fresh mud splashes on the rocks below, and the sides of the mud cups, which had begun to fall away, were beginning to be built up. I made a rough hide and spent several hours watching one of the females, as she came with mud in her beak, and usually a few fine rootlets, and smeared them onto the sides of the nest with a slight vibratory movement of the head. It seemed an ineffective way to build what ends as a heavy mud bracket, stuck onto a smooth rock wall, but almost certainly the mud is mixed with saliva which binds it together and helps to glue it to the rock. Traces of what is probably hardened saliva glisten on the rim of newly completed nests.

The first egg was laid on March 2, in the nest over the deep fissure, convenient to watch but inaccessible. The clutch was completed with the laying of a second egg two days later. By hanging a piece of cloth across the front of a low, half-dark overhang, I could sit in the darkness behind quite invisible to the incubating bird, and I could enter this simple hide without being seen by crawling along under the overhang from one side. I wanted to observe the female's behavior at the nest; to check that the male—as seemed probable—took no part in nesting duties; and most of all, if the eggs hatched, to see how the young were fed.

All our evidence suggested that the adults feed only on fruit. We had collected hundreds of regurgitated seeds from below the nests and from beside the males' courts, and had found no trace of insect remains. The seeds were nearly all from trees of the same few families whose fruit forms the staple diet of other very specialized frugivorous birds. But only observations of the feeding of the young would show whether they too were reared wholly on fruit, like the young bellbird.

The female incubated the two eggs in long spells, sometimes sitting for over two hours at a stretch. Toward the end of a session she would become restless, and then quite suddenly fly off, leaving through a narrow crack between the rocks and often giving one or two squawks, as if of relief, as she got clear of the crevice. She would return equally expeditiously, entering silently and going straight to the nest. Two other females were often about in the cave. They were usually not visible from my hide, but almost certainly they were the owners of the other two nests. Once, more surprisingly, an adult male entered the cave. He stayed for only a minute or two, perching on ledges and flying about, and his presence caused no reaction from the incubating female. We had seen an adult male associating with females in the forest near the cave, so evidently there is some social contact between the sexes away from the dancing grounds. But it seems rather likely that this particular male held no court, as the established males are almost constantly present at the dancing ground throughout the day. Since the nest gets most of its protection from its safe position there is probably less need for the sexes to keep rigidly apart from each other when the females are nesting; but there is no evidence that the males show any positive interest in the nest itself.

After twenty days of incubation I visited the nest daily, expecting an incubation period of about twenty-five days. Day after day there was no sign of hatching, and then suddenly the female deserted, for no obvious reason, after twenty-nine days of sitting. Allowing two days to make sure that she would not return, I took the eggs for examination—or rather I got William to take them, knowing that he would be more skillful than I. With a spoon tied to the end of a long pole, from a rock some 15 feet away he managed to scoop up each egg in turn from the inaccessible nest, which not only had sheer rock above it for twenty feet but overhung a deep crack about equally deep. The eggs were infertile.

After this disappointment, which came near the end of our time in the Kanukus, there was no chance of getting the information that I wanted from another nest. Eggs had been laid in one of the distant nests in mid-March, but they would not hatch before we were due to leave; the other nests were still empty. At this point Dr. Carl Hopkins of Rockefeller University, who was camping not far from us and studying the many kinds of electric fish that inhabit the rivers and creeks of the area, provided most welcome help. He agreed to check the two other nests above our camp, with William's assistance, after we had left; and he continued to do this until the end of June. Eggs were laid in both in late April, and they hatched after twenty-seven or twenty-eight days of incubation, one of the longest periods known for a passerine bird. He was less lucky with the fledging period as the young disappeared after thirty days, before they could have flown. Without doubt they were taken by local Indians, who can get a good price for a young Cock-of-the-rock in Georgetown. I had to be content with an incomplete study of the nesting of the Cock-of-the-rock.

3

The Black-and-White Manakin

There is something to be said for watching the commonest birds in your area. In England there is still a lot to be found out about the Blackbird and Song Thrush, while another very common garden bird, the Dunnock, has been so much neglected that we still do not know whether it lives conventionally, in pairs, or whether the trios of birds that one so often sees are a sign of some less usual social organization. Of course the birds have to be marked individually before any such study can make much headway, but birds are ringed annually by the hundreds of thousands for the study of migration and mortality. Most birdwatchers prefer to go further afield and look for rare birds, even though they do not find out much about them.

I was fortunate in Trinidad, for not only were the two commonest birds in the forest very little known but in appearance and behavior they were as remarkable as any two small birds that one could hope to find anywhere. Both were members of the manakin family. I began to watch them, and continued for as long as I was in Trinidad. The Golden-headed

Manakin, although the more abundant of the two, was the more difficult to get to grips with, as its displays take place well up in the trees and its nests are built higher above the ground. The Black-and-white Manakin both displays and nests close to the ground, and so I got a more intimate knowledge of it.[11]

Manakins are chickadee-sized birds, compact and stocky and with something of the verve and energy of chickadees but utterly different in all other ways. They mainly eat berries, which they seize in flight in short, rapid sallies. As if to emphasize their virtuosity in flight, the wing feathers of some species are curiously modified to make whirring or snapping sounds. When perched, they do not climb or clamber at all, or even hop from perch to perch, but for the most part only make little shuffling movements sideways along the perch.

A close relative of the Black-and-white Manakin was already well known for its courtship displays when I began my observations. Frank M. Chapman, who had earlier described the bellbird's calls in Trinidad, had late in his life studied the behavior of Gould's Manakin in Panama, and his account was so striking that it has found a place in most treatises on bird behavior.[12] The amazingly loud mechanical noises which accompanied the displays had prompted Chapman to send specimens of the males to Percy Lowe, a British anatomist. Lowe described the modifications of the flight feathers and a complicated musculature attached to the bases of the feathers, whereby the various mechanical sounds are produced.[13]

Chapman studied a group of male manakins which congregated at a traditional area in the forest undergrowth, each bird clearing a small "court" for himself by removing all leaves and debris from a small patch of ground. He described how they performed elaborate and amazingly rapid movements of a stereotyped pattern on and around their courts, accompanied by loud snapping, rattling, and whirring noises, apparently with the object of attracting females to dance with them and finally to mate. His account was very detailed in some respects but his observations were not very long continued and a good many points remained unexplained. There was obviously scope for a more thorough field study.

The group of Gould's Manakins which Chapman studied had their display ground on Barro Colorado Island, the large forested island that was formed in Gatun Lake when part of the Chagres River was flooded to form the central part of the Panama Canal. Gould's Manakin was rather rare on this island, as most of the habitat was not really suitable for it, and there was only one small display ground. By contrast, even the casual observer in the Northern Range of Trinidad is likely to become aware of Black-and-white Manakins. The white-bodied males, with their black caps, wings and tail, whir like huge grasshoppers as they fly low across the forest trails or snatch berries from some roadside bush or tree. A closer view shows them to be stocky little birds, with short wings and rather long orange legs. The white throat feathers of the male are elongated and can be puffed out so that they protrude well in front of the beak, giving the bird its other English name, White-bearded Manakin. The female's plumage is entirely olive green, but she too has orange legs.

Within the 450 acres of forest where I made my observations there were seven display grounds, at which a minimum of 205 males held courts. Three of the display grounds were within earshot of forest paths, the largest, with up to 70 courts, being just beside a regularly used trail. There were few times of the day, or of the year, when one could pass this group of males without being aware of their activities. The two display grounds especially suitable for detailed and continuous study were, however, away from paths. They were in the forest on the steep ridges on either side of the small stream which flowed down past our house, and they were only about a ten minutes' walk away. What made them even more convenient was that the males which held courts at them came down and bathed in the stream, and fed at berry-bearing bushes and small trees at the forest edge just behind the house, so that by setting mist-nests[14] near the house we could catch and ring many of these males without disturbing them at the display grounds. The females that visited the display grounds also fed and bathed along the stream, and some nested beside

Male Black-and-white Manakin, resting position

it. I only very occasionally set nets at the display grounds, in order to catch particular birds which had escaped being trapped elsewhere; otherwise they were undisturbed. I built a raised hide at one display ground, which became very dilapidated over the next four years and finally hardly hid me at all; but it did not matter by then as the birds were so tame that they ignored me. It was best not to depend too much on a hide for concealment, as sometimes I needed to watch particular birds from other positions at the display ground. The hide became a useful platform, from which I could see more of the courts on the rough sloping ground than I could from ground level. At the other display ground I simply sat quietly and watched. Before long most of the males at both display grounds were individually color-ringed, and I was able to follow some for over three years and many others for over two years.

Like Gould's Manakin, the male Black-and-white Manakin clears a small court on the forest floor. From it he removes any leaf or other light object that may land on it, darting and seizing it in his beak, much as he seizes a berry to eat, and whirring off with it without alighting and often without any noticeable pause in flight, to land a few feet away, beyond the edge of the court, and let the object drop. The whole movement is so quick that it may often be missed unless one is prepared for it; but one can easily elicit it by simply placing a dead leaf conspicuously on a bird's court. If the object is larger or less easy to move the manakin may alight beside it and tug at it, and in this way rootlets crossing the court may be stripped of their bark. Thus the manakin keeps his court as clean and as conspicuous as a patch of bare soil on ground covered with leaf litter can be, and equally importantly he makes it suitable for the acrobatics that he performs on it.

To be suitable for his display, the male must select a spot where two or more small saplings—or smooth vertical stems of some kind—are growing not more than two or three feet apart from one another; for repeated and rapid jumps between upright perches, to and fro across the court, are the main element in the display. Three or four such uprights allow some variety in the evolutions.

A typical court is two or three feet across and roughly oval, and has near its edge two or more of the required uprights. Neighboring courts may almost touch one another, but more usually they are a few feet or a few yards apart. The two display grounds which I watched most carefully had 24–28 and 30–33 courts; the exact number varied a little from year to year. Each display ground covered an area of about 30 by 20 yards. The largest display ground that I knew had about 70 courts in about the same area.

Display grounds are traditional, persisting year after year in the same place if the forest is not disturbed. Those that were near paths in the Arima Valley had been known to the local people for many years, and not one of the seven display grounds which I visited regularly for four years was abandoned or changed its position. Moreover, most of the same courts remained in use. Such constancy of occupation is only possible because the forest itself changes very slowly. The lower growth in the forest consists, for the most part, not of herbaceous plants but of saplings and young trees with bare straight stems less than an inch in diameter. If a tree falls and a gap is opened in the canopy overhead, these young trees grow up toward the light and there is a period of intense competition between them. This, at least, is what many botanists think happens, and it seems very likely to be so, but the whole process must take many years and it has apparently not been verified by direct observation. What is certain is that the young trees below the forest canopy may remain much the same size for years if there is no disturbance. In four and a half years there was no appreciable increase in the diameter of the saplings used by the manakins at the display grounds which I studied.

For most of the year, with a break of a few weeks when they are molting, and for most of each day, the adult male Black-and-white Manakins are at their courts. Almost as soon as it is light, the first males appear at the display ground, and they remain until the forest begins to darken. Every now and then they fly off to feed, usually returning after less than five minutes, since the fruits that they take are easily found and they can soon fill their stomachs. In the afternoon they bathe in some shallow stream nearby and may be away from their courts for a rather longer period. A marked individual at whose court we watched for the whole of the daylight hours was present for 90 percent of the entire time.

Unlike the Cock-of-the-rock, which spends much of its time in the trees above its court except when a female is present, the Black-and-white Manakin stays down near his court for most of the time, whether females are present or not. He displays spontaneously, especially in the early morning and the afternoon, and the display of one male stimulates others to display, so that there are bursts of great activity and periods of comparative calm, with the greatest concentrations of activity between 6:30 and 7:30 in the morning and 1:30 and 2:30 in the afternoon. The early afternoon is a dull time outside the forest, when most birds seek shelter from the heat of the sun, but in the forest it is the time when leks of cotingas and manakins rise to the second of their daily peaks of activity.

The first impression of a group of displaying manakins is bewildering. Spaced only a few feet apart—if the courts are well concentrated—a number of small black and white birds are seen leaping about and performing other acrobatics with extraordinary rapidity, within a few inches of the ground. Accompanying these movements, some of which are too rapid to follow by eye, are a variety of sharp cracks, like percussion caps exploding, rolling snaps, and whirring and grunting noises, as well as a chorus of excited high-pitched calls. Closer inspection shows that each bird is performing on and around a small area of bare soil and that two or three saplings around the edges of each cleared area are the chief perches of the displaying birds. More prolonged observation shows that the birds' bewildering evolutions can be resolved into a number of highly stereotyped movements.

The most frequently performed evolution is a rapid leaping to and fro between two of the uprights, within a foot or so of the ground. The bird perches horizontally across the upright stem, with beard jutting forward, then with a loud snap it makes a flying leap across to another upright, turning in the air so that it lands facing the way it came; then with another snap it leaps back again, and so on—snap-snap-snap, back and forth across the court.

Every now and then it varies the dance. Landing transversely on one of the uprights within a few inches of the ground, it becomes momentarily tense, with beard extended—a sloweddown film shows the bird quivering as if bracing itself for the effort—then, instead of leaping across to the opposite upright, it projects itself at lightning speed headfirst down to the ground, turns in the air to land on its feet for a split second, and with a peculiar grunting noise rockets up to land in a higher position on the perch it has just left. The whole evolution—I called it the "grunt-jump"—lasts about a third of a second. It may then do what I called its "slide down the pole": with fanning wings, and taking such short and rapid steps that it seems to slide, it moves down the perch for a foot or so and remains near the bottom of the upright for a moment, usually to resume its to-and-fro leaping and snapping.

One other less frequently seen display completes the repertoire. This I called "fanning." Unlike the displays already described, it is performed on a horizontal perch. The bird leans forward, humps up its back in a peculiar way, and rapidly beats its wings with a low-pitched whirring sound, swaying its head and body from side to side as it does so. Apparently due to the retraction of the head between the "shoulders" the feathers of the neck are pushed forward and upward each time the wings are raised so that they project

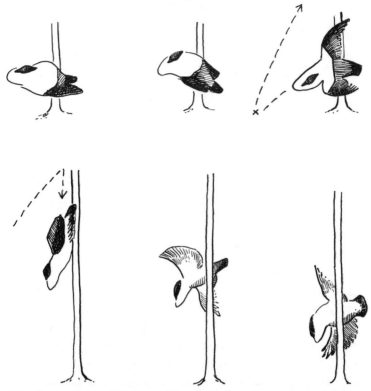

The "grunt-jump," followed by a "slide down the pole";
based on single frames of a movie film

"Fanning"; based on single frames of movie film

like two flickering white puffs at either side of the bird's head. Males usually "fan" on low perches round their courts, moving slowly from perch to perch without the explosive leaps of the main dance.

All this may be going on without a sign of any female being present. But if a female appears there is a burst of excitement; all the males in the neighborhood perform, and activity remains high as long as she is present. Early in the season females tend to visit the display grounds in small groups. They appear nervous, almost bewildered by the males' activities, and move from court to court as if at random, perching and making short flights and tending to keep loosely together. Later they appear much more purposeful; they usually come singly, go straight to a male's court, and join him in his dance. This they do by leaping back and forth across the court between the uprights, usually a few inches above the male, and timing the leaps so that their paths cross in midair. As the male approaches the upright on which the female has landed, she leaps back to the one he has left.

For several seconds they may continue crisscrossing between the perches, until the female loses interest and moves away or, if she is receptive, remains and mates with the male. Mating follows a stereotyped and most remarkable sequence. When the female lands on the special "mating sapling" she stands her ground as the male approaches. He, as usual, is keeping to a slightly lower level than she and lands below her; and then he immediately performs the "grunt-jump," leaping down to the ground and up with a grunt to a higher position on the same perch where he is now *above* the female. From this position he "slides down the perch" onto the waiting female, who remains crosswise on the vertical stem. A film that I took of this sequence showed that in the act of mating the male held on to the perch with one foot and had the other on the female's back.

The whole act is so rapid that one can easily see it in the poor light of the forest undergrowth and not realize what has happened. The movements of the cryptically colored female are much harder to follow than those of the male. When I briefly studied the displays of Gould's Manakin in Panama,

I tried to film the displays, without very satisfactory results as the light was so bad. But when I ran the film in slow motion afterward I saw that two sequences of a male "sliding down the pole," which I thought at the time he was performing *in vacuo*, in fact ended in mating. The female was just visible as she flitted off a moment after the male had left.

A constant state of rivalry and suppressed aggression persists between the males. Fights are rare, but they sometimes occur if two males are competing for the same court. The display ground at which I most often watched was on a steep slope, and occasionally rival males fought so fiercely that they lost control and rolled downhill interlocked in a black and white ball of feathers, over their neighbors' courts. Usually such fights are short-lived, and established court-holders are rarely ousted. Once, however, an outstandingly successful bird, male no. 45, who had been in occupation of his court for at least two years, had his ownership persistently contested by another male and in the end was temporarily ousted. The aggressor, though an old bird, was of unsettled habits. From March 1959, when he was trapped, to May 1960 he had held one court, abandoned it, and then disappeared for three months, presumably spending his time at another display ground, and had then reappeared and occupied another court. At the end of May he abandoned this too and began to hang about round the edges of male 45's court. On May 31 the two males were apparently involved in a fight, which unfortunately I did not see; I saw the intruding male in the afternoon at one of the usual bathing places, with the side of his head bloody and his plumage disheveled. Next morning, looking spruce again, he was in possession of male 45's court, and male 45 was not present. But a week later male 45 was back in possession. The intruding male was again hanging about round the edges of the court, and later he shifted back to one of the courts that he had occupied earlier, which he retained for over a year until my observations ceased.

Exactly as Barbara found in the bellbird, when the male manakins temporarily abandon their courts at the onset of their molt other males—often young ones—move in temporarily, but the owners regain the courts after completing their molt. At all times there is a tendency for the central courts at a display ground to be constantly occupied, while the less favored outlying courts more often fall vacant and are sometimes abandoned altogether. Thus the cohesion of the display ground is maintained.

Almost as striking as the males' mutual aggressiveness and rivalry is their sociability. Males that are contesting possession of the same court will sit for long periods within a few inches of one another at times when display and overt aggressive behavior are slack. Similarly, neighboring males have a strong tendency to perch close together on neutral ground between the courts. Often such birds leave the display ground together to feed, and return at the same time. There is little doubt that the very existence of a communal display ground such as the Black-and-white Manakin's depends on the balance between these aggressive and social tendencies.

Some of the males were much more successful than others in attracting females to their courts. As far as I could see, the position of the court was the key to success; the more central courts in the display ground were the most frequently visited by females. I could find no evidence that the males which occupied the central courts were inherently better in any way than those with peripheral courts; but it would have been impossible to recognize slight differences in the exuberance of their display, since the mere fact of having a central court, with a maximum of stimulation from surrounding males, meant that the owners spent longer at them and displayed more persistently than the more outlying males.

It has often been supposed that birds which display conspicuously in groups must dangerously expose themselves to predators; in fact, in discussions of the evolution of lek displays this supposed disadvantage has been set against the other probable advantages. For male manakins in Trinidad, however, the risk of predation at the lek must be very slight indeed. I had 38 court-holding males which were color-ringed for long enough for me to be able to record their survival over one, two, or three years, giving a total of 56 bird-years. The annual survival rate of these birds was 89 percent. Six years after we left Trinidad, Dr. Alan Lill began to study the same manakin population and he continued for four years, observing and retrapping many of my ringed birds. One of the males was still present and displaying at its court at an age of at least 14 years. A calculation of the annual survival rate of both males and females over the ten-year interval between our two periods of study showed that it was over 80 percent and probably closer to 90 percent.[15] Such high survival rates are equaled only by some long-lived sea birds in temperate regions. Small land birds at high latitudes have annual survival rates mainly in the range of 30 to 50 percent.

If the males exposed themselves to a high risk of predation by displaying so conspicuously and continually, it is almost inconceivable that they could survive as well as they do. In fact, there are no forest-living hawks in Trinidad whose main prey is small birds. There are some on the mainland of tropical America but they seem not to be very common, and in any case it is doubtful if they hunt for small birds near the ground in the thicker kind of forest undergrowth where Black-and-white Manakins display. Probably it has never been profitable for any hawk to specialize in hunting in such difficult conditions.

It is perhaps more remarkable that the manakins manage to escape all danger so successfully at night, when they roost in thick growth in the lower levels of the forest, for it is quite certain that many kinds of snakes and small predatory mammals are active at night, and the snakes destroy a high proportion of all forest nests. Our ignorance of what goes on at night in the forest is profound. As regards the manakins, all one can say is that they must possess most efficient adaptations of behavior, probably involving their selection of roosting sites and their reaction to disturbance.

The Black-and-white Manakin's nesting habits offered no challenge like the bellbird's. The nest was already well known when I began my work; although it is fairly inconspicuous it is by no means difficult to find once one knows where to look. It is a loosely woven hammocklike cup, slung in a fork of some low plant, most often between the horizontal twigs of a small sapling or the lateral frondlets of a large fern frond.

Typically it is attached to a stream-side plant and very often it overhangs the water, probably gaining extra protection thereby from ground predators.

As is to be expected, the female builds and tends the nest entirely by herself. The two eggs are covered with thick brownish mottlings and are about as well camouflaged as they can be—at least they do not add to the conspicuousness of the nest when the female is off it. Incubation takes eighteen or nineteen days, and the young remain in the nest for thirteen to fifteen days. The female feeds them, by regurgitation, on a mixed diet of insects and fruit. The fruits include the same kinds as the adults themselves eat, except for some of the largest. Even so, it is surprising to see what relatively large fruits are thrust down the nestlings' throats, some of which consist mainly of a large seed with only a thin coating of flesh. The nestlings regurgitate the larger seeds and often one or two lie in the nest cup beside them, until the female finally swallows them or carries them away. The female also swallows the nestlings' feces up to about the twelfth day. Later, the nestlings void them over the nest edge, so that an accumulation of regurgitated and defecated seeds, with a few insect hard parts, spatters the ground beneath the nest.

Adaptations promoting the inconspicuousness of the nest and its contents have not reached such perfection in the Black-and-white Manakin as in the Bearded Bellbird. The nest itself is easier to find, at least for humans. The female visits it much more often. Small nestlings make faint cheeping calls, but large nestlings seem to be quite silent. When she is off the nest the female shows her alarm by calling if one approaches too near to it; if she is on, she may give a distraction display, fluttering off the nest and away slowly and conspicuously in a labored manner, as if with a broken wing. In spite of all these precautions, only a small fraction of the nests survive to produce fledged young—out of a sample of 227 nests whose outcome I could assess, only 44 (19 percent) were successful. Snakes were probably the chief predators, but we rarely had any direct evidence; one day the nest contents were there, the next day it was clean and empty.

The nesting season is long, usually beginning early in the

year and continuing until about July. Females nest repeatedly in the course of the season; they often build a new nest close to the previous one, or even reuse the old nest. By following the succession of nests of a number of birds I found that each female nests on average about three times in a season; one bird nested as many as five times. In spite of these repeated efforts, the manakins do not breed very prolifically. Each nest resulted on average in about one-third of a young bird reaching the flying stage. If three is taken as the average number of nesting attempts, each female thus produced on average one flying young each year. I ringed a number of nestlings, and found that after they had left the nest about one-third of them survived until they were adult. Thus it seems that each breeding female contributes on average about one-third of a bird per year to the adult population.

For no very obvious reason, the start of the breeding season varied considerably from year to year. In one year nesting began at the end of December, in another in February, in two years in April, and in one year hardly any nesting began until May. Fluctuations in the supply of readily available fruit were probably the main cause. Altogether I recorded over a hundred different kinds of fruit in the manakins' diet, but some kinds were much more important than others. The elderberry-like fruits of the family Melastomaceae were easily the most important, both in variety and in quantity. At least seventeen different species of melastomes were among the food recorded. The Rubiaceae, with fifteen species, was second, but the quantities taken were probably much smaller than the quantities of melastomes.

A regular supply of these fruits was available throughout the year; the melastomes alone produced a year-round succession of ripe fruits. But the supply was not constant; it showed regular seasonal fluctuations. The greatest numbers of different fruits were available during the manakins' breeding season (March to June). From December—a seasonal low point—to March there was an increase in the variety of the fruit supply, but it was not a regular and predictable increase. In one year there was an unusual shortage of fruit in March, and the manakins temporarily abandoned their courts. It was not possible to be certain, for it is very difficult to keep a detailed and accurate record of the amount of food available to a bird in an area of rich forest, but it looked as if the start of breeding depended mainly on this seasonal increase in fruit supplies. Perhaps at some critical level it enabled the females to accumulate the necessary energy reserves to begin to build a nest and produce eggs.

The availability of nest material may also have had some effect. For its nest lining, the manakins use the branching panicles of *Nepsera aquatica*, a small herbaceous member of the Melastomaceae. The brown stalks of these panicles are very fine, smooth, and shiny; each of the branches into which they are subdivided ends in a small fruit capsule. Thus the panicles adhere to each other when they are pressed together, so that if the lining is pulled it usually comes away from the rest of the nest intact. Many of the manakins in my study area had to fly considerable distances to find *Nepsera*, which grows in the open on forest edges and roadsides. I trapped six birds which had nest material in their beaks when they flew into the nets, and in each case it was *Nepsera* that they were carrying. In the one year when nesting began very early, *Nepsera*, a seasonal plant, had not yet fruited and the manakins lined their early nests with fine dead grasses, which did not hold together nearly so well and made the nest cup more conspicuous. Unfortunately there were few of these early nests, and in any case most nests as usual failed, so I could not tell whether the less suitable nest-lining reduced the chances of successful breeding.

4

The Blue-Backed Manakins: Courtship by Duets and Trios

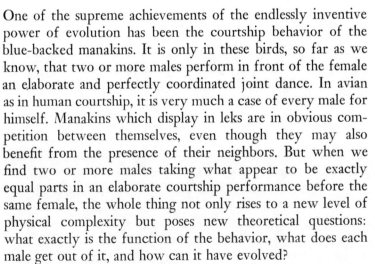

One of the supreme achievements of the endlessly inventive power of evolution has been the courtship behavior of the blue-backed manakins. It is only in these birds, so far as we know, that two or more males perform in front of the female an elaborate and perfectly coordinated joint dance. In avian as in human courtship, it is very much a case of every male for himself. Manakins which display in leks are in obvious competition between themselves, even though they may also benefit from the presence of their neighbors. But when we find two or more males taking what appear to be exactly equal parts in an elaborate courtship performance before the same female, the whole thing not only rises to a new level of physical complexity but poses new theoretical questions: what exactly is the function of the behavior, what does each male get out of it, and how can it have evolved?

There are four species of blue-backed manakins and between them they cover a great part of the tropical forest areas of America. But they are rather hard to watch; they usually perform in thick undergrowth and they do not like to be watched at close quarters; consequently the full sequence of their displays is not likely to be seen except by a persistent observer who has plenty of time to spare and is willing to put up with many disappointing sessions in the hope of a few rewarding ones. For these reasons there have been few good descriptions of their displays, which have usually been only briefly seen by a lucky chance.

The most widespread species, usually known simply as the Blue-backed Manakin, is found over much of northern South America, and has an outlying population in Tobago, Trinidad's small sister-island. It is one of a small number of birds that for no obvious reason occur in Tobago, which lies out beyond Trinidad further from the mainland, but misses out Trinidad itself. It is a rather large manakin, as also are its relatives, about the size of a House Sparrow but of the usual stocky manakin build. The males are black with a flat scarlet skullcap, a skyblue back, and pale orange legs, a most distinguished combination. The skullcap is roughly triangular in shape and consists of elongated, glossy feathers. Females have the usual uniform olive green plumage, and pale orange legs.

When I first visited Trinidad for a few weeks in 1956, I went over to Tobago for a week and spent most of my time watching the Blue-backed Manakins in the forest near the top of Pigeon Peak, the highest point at the north end of the island. I stayed in comfort at the Bird of Paradise Inn down by the shore and walked up early each morning. In June 1958, after our wedding, we returned to our house in the Arima Valley as the birds' breeding season was in full swing and there was no better place to be; but when things became slacker, in July, we went over to Tobago for a week and had a rather unconventional honeymoon. We spent most of the time camping on the top of Pigeon Peak, to try to see more of the manakins. Our camping equipment was of the simplest; we had no tent but only a single very wide hammock, and the rain poured down, as it so often does on the Main Ridge of Tobago. Not surprisingly, we did not see as much of the manakins' displays as I had seen in the dry season two years earlier; neither, incidentally, can we recommend a single hammock for two people, even on a honeymoon. In particular, we failed to see the final phases of the manakins' courtship dance, which I was sure must culminate in mating, and without this several points remained most puzzling. In 1959 we planned things a bit better. In March, at what we thought should be the right time of year—for no occupied nest of this manakin had yet been found in Tobago— we took a cine camera and tape recorder, and stayed for a fortnight at the Bird of Paradise Inn, determined to concentrate on a small group of manakins which we had been told could be seen only a few minutes' walk from the house. This was our most successful visit. We found the manakins where they had been seen before, saw all the stages of courtship, and filmed and tape-recorded them.[16] As usual, it proved that the best policy is to concentrate on the birds on one's doorstep.

But there remained an important point which needed clarification. We had repeatedly found several males in attendance at each display site which we had watched, but without marking the birds individually we had not been able to work out their social organization. It seemed probable that the birds that performed at one perch were not all of equal status; there was probably a social hierarchy, with one male dominant, but we were not certain. So in July 1961 we returned for a final visit to Tobago. This time we watched the birds at the same place as in 1959 for two days, to see the general situation, then we concentrated on mist-netting them. We caught two, including the bird which appeared to be dominant; but we were apparently too late in the season, display was slack, and the ringed birds did not come back to the display perch; probably they were soon to begin their molt and the shock of being trapped was too much for them. Other birds came and displayed a little, but our main questions remained unanswered.

Our visit to southern Guyana in 1970 gave me a final chance to settle the question of the Blue-backed Manakin's social organization, for a group of males had a display ground very near our camp. This time I was partially successful, but I devoted only a fraction of my time to the manakins and my results were not as complete as I should have liked.[17] I think that I know how these remarkable birds organize their courtship dances, as the following account will show, but I hope that somebody with more time will go and make a really thorough study. It should not be too difficult.

Male Blue-backed Manakins advertise themselves by calling loudly at some height in the trees, but their dances take place on low perches near the forest floor. Like the display perches of other manakins, these perches continue to be used year after year, as long as the forest is undisturbed and the undergrowth remains suitable. Typically they are two to four feet above the ground, horizontal or nearly so, or convexly bowed, and they must have an adequate length uncluttered by side twigs or foliage. Between bouts of display the birds peck at the bark, which they also wear smooth with their continual perching and hopping, and they pick in flight at the leaves surrounding the perch, thereby keeping it open. In Tobago the display perches were not in very thick patches of undergrowth and were more easily watched than those in Guyana, which were all well within patches of particularly dense and twiggy undergrowth.

Just as the full dance needs the cooperation of two males, so the advertising calls can only be given in full by two males calling in unison. One male, however, initiates the performance, and all my evidence suggested that this was done by the dominant male of the group, and that it was this bird who effectively "owned" the dancing perches.

For much of the day the male is present in the trees near his dancing perches, calling intermittently. The main call is a loud, rolling churr followed by one or more incisive notes— "wwrrrr, chup" or "wwrrrr, chup-chup." The function of this call is to attract another male. Eventually one comes and joins the calling bird; the two sit together, often side by side almost touching one another, and they break into a synchronized series of "chups" (the second element of the male's summoning call) in groups usually of two, three, or four: "chup-chup, chup-chup-chup, . . ." and so on, which ring through the forest, as one observer put it, like the clicking of billiard balls. When one watches a single male uttering his invitation call over and over again, and he is then joined by another male, whereupon both break into a resounding chorus, one receives the strong impression that the solitary male is eager to utter the longer, louder phrases but simply cannot do so without the cooperation of another bird.

The ringing quality of the "chup-chups" uttered by two birds in unison apparently depends on the fact that they do not synchronize their calls exactly. A sound spectrogram that I had made showed that one bird began his calls about 0.04 or 0.05 second before the other.[18] It also showed another interesting point, that the bird which began first was the one who previously had been uttering the invitation call, the "wwrrrr, chup," on his own.

It is remarkable that the second bird can follow the duet leader so exactly, since the latter may utter anything from one to five "chups" per phrase, though two or three are the commonest numbers. Almost certainly this is done by detecting the very slight preliminary movements associated with each call. Once when I saw two birds come together, they began to call while they were still several yards apart and continued to do so for some time. At this unusual distance the calls were very poorly synchronized.

After a bout of synchronized calling, both males are likely to fly down to the display perch and the next stage of the display begins, the coordinated dance. The basic element of the dance is a fluttering jump. The bird crouches a little, then jumps up a few inches with fluttering wings, head pointing down and legs dangling, and hangs momentarily in the air, before landing back on the perch. During the jump, it utters a drawn-out vibrant "aarr-r-r-r" with the beak wide open, somewhat like the twanging of a Jew's harp.

The two males jump alternately, timing their movements perfectly so that one jumps as the other lands. They jump side by side, often with a turn in the air to land facing the other way; sometimes one jumps over the other. The timing is perfect but the orientation of the jumps is variable. As long as the males are by themselves on the perch the dance does not reach its full development; for this, the presence of a female is needed. Very often, however, a female comes to the perch

Two males engaged in a joint dance; one hovering at the
top of his jump, the other waiting for his turn to jump when
his companion lands; detail from a movie film

at about the same time as the males. In fact, it is often the
presence of a female nearby which induces the males to fly
down to the display perch in the first place.

As soon as a female lands on the display perch, normally
at the higher end of it if it is sloping, the males turn and face
her. They then begin to dance in a Catherine wheel before
her. The male nearest her first jumps fluttering into the air
in the usual way. As he does so the second male hitches himself forward on the perch, crouching, to take his place, while
the first male moves back a little in the air, to land behind the
other. As he comes down, the second male goes up, and so it
goes on. They revolve in front of the female, the perfect
rhythm of the dance emphasized by the repeated "aarr-r-r-r,
aarr-r-r-r, aarr-r-r-r . . ," the notes coming alternately from
each bird as it jumps.

It is this rhythmic twanging of a pair of dancing males
which usually leads one to the perch when one is searching
for new dancing places in the forest undergrowth—an exciting

and yet a tantalizing sound, for so many times as I have approached the source of the sound, even before glimpsing the birds through the undergrowth, they have taken alarm, stopped the dance, and vanished into the trees above.

The dance in front of a female may continue, with short breaks, for several minutes on end. If she retreats backward up the perch, as sometimes happens, the males hop up further when on the perch and do not move back so much in flight, so that the wheeling pair moves up the perch after the retreating bird. If, as I occasionally saw, the female is aggressive and moves toward the pair, they retreat down the perch, still dancing. If the female is nervous and flies to another perch a few feet away, the pair of dancing males may follow her and continue jumping in front of her; but if she moves further away they do not follow but either stop jumping or return and continue the dance on the main perch.

All bouts of jumping, whether in front of a female or by two males on their own, usually become faster and more frenzied as they go on. The jumps become lower and succeed one another more rapidly, until the birds are hardly leaving the perch and the alternate rhythmic twanging degenerates into confused bleating sounds. The last jump of all is often especially frenzied; the bird turns its body rapidly from side to side as it flutters and utters a loud bleating call with its beak especially wide open. Then two or three quite different, sudden, and very sharp notes are uttered, and at the same instant the jumping stops and the birds fly off. The birds' movements at this stage are so fast and confusing that I found it difficult to be certain, but thought it probable, that the sharp notes were always given by the bird who had just uttered the last loud bleating note, that is to say, by the last bird to jump. In any case, it seems very definitely to be a signal bringing the dance to an end.

I have referred to the third bird, to whom the dance is directed, as the female, and it very often is a female; but often too an immature male plays this part. These birds are usually recognizable by traces of adult plumage among the green, especially the red skullcap which is the first adult feature to appear. I never saw a fully adult male take the female's part, or even a nearly adult male; so it is probable that in the absence of a female only a male that is low in the social hierarchy has the appropriate behavior to act as a substitute.

Once one has found an active display perch and a good point of vantage for watching the birds without disturbing them—not always easy, since the tangled undergrowth often conceals them almost completely from more than a very few yards away—and if the season is right, the Catherine wheel dance may be seen time and time again; but it is seldom, in my experience, that one sees the next stage of the display. Indeed I did not see it in full until my third visit to Tobago, in 1959. Without this third stage, the whole performance was mystifying. The joint dance was obviously courtship, analogous to the displays of other manakins. I felt sure that mating must take place on the perch on which the birds danced, for in all the other birds with elaborate courtships on traditional perches that I knew of the display perch was also the mating perch. But how did the pair of male Blue-backed Manakins proceed at the end of their joint dance, in which, until the last moments, they had taken exactly equal parts? It was not until 1972, when I saw the display of the Blue Manakin in southeastern Brazil, the most wonderful of all displays, that the answer to this question was suggested. The last moments of the Catherine wheel dance are in fact critical; I shall return to them later in this chapter, when I describe the Blue Manakin's courtship. We did not see this clearly in the Tobago birds, but on our visit in 1959 we had as good views of the third and final stage of the courtship as we could ever hope to have.

We saw the culmination of the display on March 30 and 31, and it turned out to be quite different from anything we had seen before. We saw long sequences of display between an adult male and a female on and around the usual perch, which culminated in mating six times.

It began when a female suddenly appeared on the display perch. The male, who was nearby, proceeded to flutter around her with a butterflylike floating flight, crossing and recrossing the display perch, every second or so alighting momentarily on a perch and flying on again with a buoyant, bouncing motion. In flight his wings were well extended and appeared to move with rapid, shallow beats, and his beak was open, though no sound was uttered. If he alighted on the display perch itself, or on some other perch near the female, he would face her, crouch for a moment with head lowered, so that the blue patch on his back was exhibited, and vibrate his folded wings. As his head came down, the red cap was presented squarely to the female, appearing shieldlike as the feathers splayed out with the long lateral feathers projecting like little horns at each side. The female was thus presented with a scarlet shield surrounded by black and surmounted by a vibrating patch of sky blue. Sometimes when the male stopped in the course of his bouncing flight and faced the female, he did not adopt this posture but merely crouched, with wings flicking. Several times in the course of the display, and on both days, he flew out to a special perch some twenty feet from the main perch, in a direction in which he did not otherwise go, uttered a low twanging "quaaa" on the perch, then, with a soft but distinct click of the wings as he took off, flew back to the display perch and resumed the bouncing flight.

The female, for her part, crouched with her plumage sleeked and continually turned to face the male, clearly fascinated by his performance. Sometimes she sidled quickly along the perch, sometimes she seemed to retreat a little, but for almost the whole time she remained on the main display perch, intently watching the male as he weaved his patterns about her.

Mating followed a set pattern. The male flew in from one side and landed for a moment on a perch near the female. He then jumped onto the display perch, landing beside the female and turning in the air so that he faced the same way as she, and mounted.

This marvelous performance differed in almost every way from the Catherine wheel dance. The two most striking general differences were that only one male was involved, and that the display was quite silent except for the occasional low "quaaa" and soft click made when the male flew in from the outlying perch. During the performance no other males were seen or even heard nearby, though at least one other adult

The premating display; the male crouches, presenting the red shield of his crest to the female, who watches intently; detail from a movie film

male and two immatures had been displaying on this perch a few minutes before and displayed on it shortly afterwards. Thus we failed to find out how the dominant male—for it must have been he that mated with the female—managed to keep the other males at a distance during the vital third phase of the courtship.

I never again saw this final stage of the courtship in full. On later occasions I saw the buoyant, bouncing flight around the perch performed briefly by an adult male, with an immature male taking the female's part, as in the Catherine wheel dance, and several times I saw two adult males together crisscrossing the display perch with the bouncing flight, with no female present; but these were not long sustained. Seen in isolation they would have been misleading. Birds with elaborate and stereotyped displays often perform them partially and briefly in circumstances that are to some extent inappropriate, and there is a danger of mistaking their real function if they are seen thus out of context.

So far, I have simplified my account by writing as though each group of males had one display perch. In fact the situation was not as simple as this. The manakins on Pigeon Peak were found throughout the forest, and I watched many display perches. I had no marked birds, and so could not find out how the males were organized socially, but I thought it possible that each male owned a display perch, and that neighboring males visited the owner for the joint dances at his perch, perhaps at other times attracting him to come and dance at theirs. Down near the Bird of Paradise Inn there were fewer manakins, as only a small patch of suitable forest remained. In addition to the main display perch at which we watched, some display went on occasionally at two other perches nearby. But, as far as we could tell, there was never display at two perches at the same time, so that it seemed most likely that there was one group of males with a choice of three display perches, one of which—the one at which we watched—was the most favored.

It was obviously important to understand the males' social organization. If each adult male owned its own perch, to which it attracted other males, at least each of them had a chance of mating; though even so it might seem odd that a male should join its neighbor in the first stages of its display, neglecting its own perch to do so. If on the other hand all the males in a group ranged over a number of display perches, the situation was very different. In this case the question to be asked was whether there was a social hierarchy within the group, ensuring that only one male, the one at the top, normally had a chance to mate, or whether there was some sort of free-for-all.

It was in order to settle these points that we returned, unsuccessfully, to the Tobago manakins for a last visit in 1961, too late in the season when the birds were already ceasing to display. When we went to southern Guyana for three months in 1970, to study cotingas, and camped in the forest at the foot of the Kanuku Mountains, one of the main attractions of the camp site, for me, was that a group of Blue-backed Manakins had their display area on a patch of level ground thickly grown with secondary forest, just on the other side of the stream beside which we camped. I had what was almost certainly going to be my last chance.

These manakins were more difficult to watch than the Tobago birds. Their advertising calls were often given from one of the few very high trees in the area, and the display perches were in the thickest patches of twiggy undergrowth. But even before I had finished my trapping it was fairly clear that the group of males was behaving as a unit and the five display perches which I located were not owned by five different males. The display perches were all within earshot from a central point, and I never heard males displaying at more than one perch at a time. Sometimes, when they were alarmed by my presence near one display perch, they would fly off and begin to display at another. This made the trapping difficult, and it was some weeks before I had caught five males and decided to stop trapping and watch them. Display was never as intense as I would have liked—it may have been too early in the season—and I never saw the third phase of courtship except in a weak and incomplete form. All the displays and calls seemed identical to those of the Tobago birds.

The male which appeared to be dominant in the group had unfortunately escaped being trapped, but in spite of this the situation seemed clear. There were apparently six or seven males associated with the display perches—the five that I had ringed, two of which were in mainly juvenile plumage, the unringed adult, and perhaps another adult. The unringed adult spent much of his time uttering the summoning call from high in the trees above the display perches, and on several occasions I saw him joined by one of the other males. With the unringed bird giving the lead, the pair would then break into a bout of synchronized calling, the "chup-chup, chup-chup-chup," and might later fly down to one of the display perches and begin to dance. If the pair was disturbed at one display perch they sometimes, as already mentioned, flew directly to another one and continued their display. The unringed adult certainly went to three of the perches that were in use and probably to a fourth (the fifth perch was not seen to be visited after I finished trapping). On all the occasions when I was able to observe the relations between it and another male it was dominant, in the sense that it called up the other bird and initiated any movement from one display site to another or from a high perch down to one of the low perches.

The two younger males that were seen most frequently after being ringed each also went to three of the four display perches, either when called up by the adult male or of their own accord if they were alone.

In short, the birds were organized as a group, an adult bird was the leader, and it seemed probable that the younger birds took part in the displays as and when they were able to do so in the absence of birds dominant to them. No doubt the Tobago birds which we watched were organized in the same way, since the behavior of the two populations, about six hundred miles apart, seemed identical.

The Blue Manakin of Southeastern Brazil

In the older literature on the birds of the wooded mountains that extend along the coast of southeastern Brazil, in the general area of Rio de Janeiro and São Paulo, there are a few brief accounts of the dancing behavior of the Blue Manakin.[19] Few ornithologists had seen the dances, but they were well enough known to the local people to have given the bird the name "dançador." The accounts were partly fanciful and partly based on hearsay, but even if they were only half true they suggested that the Blue Manakin has an even more elaborate and wonderful display than the Blue-backed. One account described the males as perched in a line in front of the female, and each one in turn fluttering up to her, "kissing" her, and flying back to the end of the queue. More than one account mentioned a "master of ceremonies" who uttered special calls to start and stop the dance.

At first I thought of these accounts as the tallest of travelers' tales; but when I had seen the male Tobago manakins in their pairs fluttering up in front of the female in the Catherine wheel dance, and had heard the sharp call which brought the display to an end, I realized that the Brazilian bird might really do something like what it had been said to do. If several males were involved instead of only two, the Tobago bird's display could be changed into something not so very different from what was attributed to the Blue Manakin, allowing for some fanciful interpretation and the usual difficulty of making out exactly what is happening when one briefly sees a complex piece of behavior for the first time.

Since these early published accounts the Blue Manakin has been surprisingly neglected. Two more brief descriptions of its display appeared in 1925 and 1959,[20] but a number of discrepancies remained. I read all that I could find on these Brazilian manakins when I became interested in the Tobago birds and, inevitably, to see the display of the Blue Manakin became one of my ornithological ambitions. I did not seriously think that I ever would, but in 1972 the opportunity came. My main interest had temporarily shifted to the cotingas, and with Derek Goodwin, a colleague at the Museum, I was able to spend a few weeks in southeastern Brazil in order to study some little known species of cotingas that are confined to the forest-covered mountains where the Blue Manakin also lives.

In the beautiful Serra dos Orgãos, the "Organ Mountains," not far inland from Rio de Janeiro, whose sheer rock pinnacles with fluted organ-pipe columns rise up from steep, thickly forested valleys, we saw the manakins, but they were not very common and we found no display areas. From there we moved to the Boraceia forest reserve in the mountains between São Paulo and the sea. In this tract of forest, the wettest that I have ever tried to work in, Blue Manakins were common, and we finally managed to see their dance.

The male Blue Manakin is an outstandingly beautiful bird and a delight to watch even when it is doing nothing. In size and build it is much like the Blue-backed Manakin, but the central pair of tail feathers are elongated into a point which projects about an inch beyond the others. The wings and tail, and most of the head and neck, are black; but instead of merely a sky blue patch on the back the whole of the body is a soft powder blue of a shade most unusual in birds. And instead of a red skullcap of feathers which lie flat, there is a fiery red cap of short upstanding feathers like plush. Brilliant enough when seen under any ordinary light, seen against the sun, as they sometimes are when one looks up at the bird in the forest, these feathers glow with transmitted light.

We had spent several days working in the dripping Boraceia forest, which most of the time was wrapped in a Scotch mist from which a steady drizzle descended, so that even the treetops were barely visible, and had been trying without much success to see and study the Bare-throated Bellbird and the Hooded Berry-eater, failing entirely to find a third species, the Shrike-like Cotinga. Every half mile or so along the trails we would pass within earshot of groups of Blue Manakins uttering their very loud advertising calls, a sort of confused gabbling very unlike the synchronized "chup-chups" of the Tobago birds, from the thick foliage of high trees. Occasionally we heard at some distance the twanging, identical to that of the Tobago birds, which indicated that they were down in the undergrowth, dancing. We decided in the end that we could not go on ignoring these sounds, and for the last few days of our stay we devoted half our time to the manakins. Even so, we saw very little display; but what we did see compensated for many hours of waiting and seeing nothing.

The birds spent a great deal of time giving their loud calls from high in trees. They were very difficult to see, but apparently did not sit side by side very close to each other when calling, as male Blue-backed Manakins do. My tape recordings showed that at least two, and at times almost certainly three or more birds, participated in the gabbling chorus, in which the basic note was a quick disyllable. It is probably because more than two birds participate, and because they do not sit very close to each other when doing so, that Blue Manakins do not give their advertising calls in perfect unison as Blue-backed Manakins do.

The low perches on which they danced were typically in very thick undergrowth, very much like the kind of places in which our Blue-backed Manakins danced in Guyana. And the rhythmic twanging call, uttered as the birds jumped, sounded exactly the same. When, one morning at about 8 o'clock, I finally managed to track down a group of dancing birds and get sight of them without their seeing me and stopping—as usually happened—I was able to do so only because the undergrowth *was* so thick. They were performing in the middle of an impenetrable tangle of woody undergrowth, matted with vines and with thick young bamboo round the edge. Since the surrounding area was a little lighter and more open, the outer wall of this great clump was screened with leaves, which effectively hid me from the birds as I approached. When I reached the edge of the clump it was obvious from the tantalizing Jew's harp twanging, which was going on and on, that the birds were within a few yards of me. At first I could see nothing, but by lying flat on the ground and carefully parting the twigs and leaves to make a small hole I was able to look into the clump, and saw the birds, still at their dance, so close that I was only just able to focus my field glasses on them.

The dance went on, with occasional short breaks, for about ten minutes, and then there was a longer break. I stayed, and later in the morning the birds came back and danced again. When the display seemed to have temporarily finished I carefully made a better hole in the screening vegetation, a few feet from my original observation point, giving me a clearer view of the display perch, and I returned in the afternoon to watch again. The males came back, and a female was with them on the perch for most of the time. I was able to see many marvelous sequences of display without in the least disturbing the birds.

On other days I saw some fragmentary bits of display elsewhere, and Derek Goodwin saw one very good dancing sequence at another place. What seems to be the most reliable of the accounts published previously agrees in every detail with what we saw, as far as it goes. Thus I feel confident that what I saw was typical, and that future ornithologists will confirm it—though I am also sure that anybody who has the opportunity to make more thorough observations will add significantly to this account.

The events leading up to a bout of dancing were hard to observe, and I do not know what was the usual sequence. Sometimes a male, after calling from a high perch, came down to the display perch and spent some time there by himself, uttering the loud summoning calls. Sometimes, like the Blue-backed Manakin, a single male gave an occasional jump up and down, accompanied with the twanging call. The impression was that he was trying to call up other birds so that the proper dance could begin. Usually all the males appeared at about the same time, after they had spent some time calling excitedly in the trees above.

In all the bouts of dancing that we saw, three males and a single female took part. These males came to the perch in quick succession; the female was either on the perch already, or very near it. The dancing began the moment they were assembled; the order of the dance was always the same.

The males crouch in a compact row, all facing the same way; the female is by herself a foot or so away on the same perch. Then the male nearest her jumps up with fluttering wings, utters the twanging "aarr-r-r-r," and moves back to the end of the line. The other males, crouching and quivering as they take little side steps along the perch, move towards the female, and as the first male lands the one now at the head of the line jumps, moves back in the air, and so on. With their red caps glowing, they form a whirling torch in front of the female, who perches motionless, watching them, or betrays slight nervousness by an occasional quick flick of her wings. As the dance proceeds the rhythm becomes more rapid, and the jumps lower. The twanging calls become less distinct; they run together and take on a frenzied, bleating quality. Now, as each bird jumps, instead of at once moving back to the end of the queue, it first moves forward a few inches until it is hovering almost over the female, where it remains for a moment looking down at her, before moving back to the end of the line. As though the Catherine wheel has been squashed from above, the jumping birds as they move to the back pass low in front of the waiting males and not over their backs, as at the beginning of the bout.

The end of the dance is very sudden, and the ritual at first takes one so completely by surprise that it needs watching a few times before one is sure exactly what has happened. One of the males, as he hovers before the female, instead of the twanging "aarr-r-r-r" utter a rapid "flup-flup-flup"—a noise

The Blue Manakin's Catherine wheel dance

which sounds as if it might be made by the wings but is almost certainly vocal—then a moment later, still hovering, gives a very sharp, penetrating "zeek-eek-eek," and immediately flies off to a perch a few feet away. At the sound of the "zeek-eek-eek" the other two males crouch absolutely motionless and remain still for a second or two after, and then they too fly off to perches nearby. The female normally remains on the perch.

Sometimes when I saw it, the last but one of the males to jump also uttered the "flup-flup-flup," but he then went back to the end of the line in the usual way. This seems to act as a preliminary announcement of the impending end of the dance, but it is always the "zeek-eek-eek" which actually brings the dance to a close. The whole sequence is almost as striking to hear as it is to see. Several times I heard the unmistakable sounds from birds that were quite out of sight, and knew just what I was missing—the rhythmic twanging speeding up to a frenzied bleating, the change of note ending with the sharp "zeeks," and then silence.

Usually, after the end of a bout of dancing, the males would fly back to the perch after a short interval and the dance would begin again. But once the routine was changed and I saw the next phase of courtship, corresponding exactly to the third phase of display of the Tobago manakin. After the last dance the male which had uttered the "zeek-eek-eek" remained crouching on the perch to which he had flown, flicking his wings. He then began to make buoyant, floating flights round the female, who remained crouching on the perch. When the male landed between flights he crouched, but unlike the Blue-backed Manakin, which holds its head down at this point and presents its red skullcap like a shield to the female, he held his head up with crown feathers raised, so that the brilliant cap transmitted the light. He landed mostly on adjacent perches but sometimes on the same perch as the female; but he did not mount. Finally the female flew off, and the male then flew to the perch she had left and with legs stretched did several rapid side-to-side "slides" of about three inches each way—actually very quick side-stepping with short steps, but done so rapidly that he appeared to slide. He then flew off too and the whole display sequence came to an end.

This performance provided the key to something that I had always found puzzling in the Tobago manakin. All three phases of courtship display are basically similar in the two species, with the main difference that in the Blue Manakin three males (or perhaps sometimes more) take part and in the Blue-backed Manakin only two. The Blue-backed Manakin's Catherine wheel dance ends with the same sharp "zeek-eek-eek"; but I had never seen the transition from this to the third phase, in which a single male weaves his floating flight round the female. In the Blue Manakin, watching from a few yards away and keeping my eyes on each bird as it jumped, I could see quite clearly what happened. The male which gave the last jump uttered as he did so the short burst of sharp calls. This call seemed to petrify the other two males; they crouched motionless for a second, then left the perch. The male who had called merely flew to another perch a few feet away, then came back for the final phase of the courtship, while the two others remained at a distance. He had, literally, cleared the court, as clearly as if he had said "That's enough. I don't need your help any more. Now clear off!" I have no doubt that he was the dominant male of the group.

There were several differences, mainly slight, in the performances of the Blue Manakins from those that I had seen of the Blue-backed in addition to the main difference in the number of males taking part. One difference was that, as the Blue Manakins' Catherine wheel dance became more rapid and frenzied, each male hovered for a moment almost over the female and very close to her before moving back to the end of the line. In the third phase of courtship the single male, as he moved in bouncing flight round the female, exhibited his flaming crest to best advantage, whenever he landed, by holding his head up so that the light shone through it, whereas the Blue-backed male presents his duller but more strikingly shaped cap squarely to the female. A notable difference resulted from the different behavior of the other males during this third phase. When the Blue-backed male performed his floating flight round the female, the display was quite silent except for the low "quaaa" and the soft wing-click as he flew in from the outlying perch. But on the only occasion when I saw the Blue Manakin at this stage of its courtship, the males which he had dismissed to the sidelines—and perhaps some other males too—remained perching not many yards away calling excitedly, evidently watching the performance.

One must see a display of this sort again and again, and at different times and in different places, to record all the possible variations in sequence and in the roles of the individual birds participating. But all our experience of manakins and cotingas has shown that the complex display movements themselves are highly stereotyped. There are no detectable individual variations in performance, and the ability to perform the movements appropriate to its species and to coordinate them with the movements of other individuals must be innate in each bird. But there *is* variation in the roles played by different individuals, and in the intensity and completeness with which display sequences are performed; and if the display is complex this may lead to confusing variations in performance, if only a few bouts of display are seen.

Uncertainty remains regarding one important point, the number of males that may participate in the Catherine wheel dance. Each time we saw it three males took part, although sometimes there were certainly more males in the immediate vicinity. The most detailed and recent of the earlier accounts also all refer to three males. On the other hand some of the older accounts mention larger numbers, and since the Blue Manakin is free from the restriction which seems to limit the Blue-backed Manakin's performance to a duet—the exactly synchronized calling of two males, and their exactly timed alternate jumping on the display perch—there seems no reason why any number of males should not take part.

Several males in a row in front of the female; each flying up and kissing the female before flying back to the end of the line; a master of ceremonies who gives the signal to start and then to stop the dance; the unlikely sounding traveler's tale is correct in its essentials, if one counts the summoning call as the signal to start the dance, and the male hovering just over the female, and looking down at her as she looks up, as kissing. It is not a bad description if one considers that it was probably based on a brief chance encounter without benefit of field glasses.

5

*Some Consequences of
Eating Fruit*

Most small or medium-sized birds living in forests depend on
two main sources of food: insects and fruit. A good many eat
insects only; a smaller number eat only fruit; most eat some
insects and some fruit. Nectar is a third important source of
food, but it is exploited by only a few specialized kinds of
birds. All sorts of consequences follow once a species has begun to concentrate on one of these basic types of diet. Here I
shall consider first the consequences of making a choice between insects and fruit, and then the further consequences of
increasing specialization on a diet of fruit.[21]

Insects are hard to find—except for distasteful ones, which
may make themselves positively conspicuous with warning
colors and sluggish behavior. Indeed, the more they are preyed
on the better their adaptations for escape and concealment
become, because the pressure from predators is the selective
force that perfects these adaptations. Insects are also very
diverse, and the ways in which they conceal themselves are
innumerable. As a consequence, special searching and catching
techniques are needed for the efficient exploitation of insects

for food, and different techniques are needed for different kinds of insects. All this means that insect-eaters tend to be specialists, and a complex tropical forest can support many kinds of them, none of which is likely to be very abundant.

For a fruit-eater the situation is very different. It is by being eaten by birds (and some other animals) that the seeds of many fruits are dispersed. To put it in the simplest terms, insects do not want to be eaten, but fruit does. Consequently fruit is not concealed; it advertises itself, and the more it is "preyed on" and its seeds are dispersed the more abundant it is likely to become. It will usually be an advantage, too, for a fruit to be eaten by as many different kinds of birds as possible. Thus whereas insects have many different ways of being inconspicuous, fruit tends to be conspicuous in a limited number of ways and to be accessible to many different kinds of birds. In consequence, fruits do not offer their eaters as many different opportunities for specialization as insects do, and so the number of fruit-eating species is smaller than the number of insect-eaters. For example, there are only 79 species of cotingas and 59 species of manakins, but in the related family of tyrant-flycatchers, which are nearly all insectivorous, there are 365 species, and in the exclusively insectivorous ovenbird and antbird families of the New World tropics there are 215 and 222 species respectively.[22]

Although the number of fruit-eating species is considerably smaller than the number of insect-eaters, fruit-eaters tend to be individually abundant, presumably because of the special property of their food supply mentioned above, that it tends to be abundant and easily exploited. Thus, in the Trinidad forest where we worked, the two manakins were the most abundant species, while the small flycatchers, birds of about the same size and living in the same habitat, were all much less numerous. In the nets that we set at a few regular trapping places near our house we caught 471 different Golden-headed Manakins and 246 different Black-and-white Manakins; the combined total of 11 species of flycatchers did not reach even the latter figure.

In addition to these general consequences of eating insects or fruit, the diet may profoundly influence the social organization of a species. This is a consequence of the difference in spatial distribution between insects and fruits. Insects are more or less evenly, but thinly, distributed through the environment; fruit on the other hand is irregularly clumped, and the position of the clumps in any small area is continually changing as the fruit ripens on one tree and another loses its fruit. Consequently insectivorous birds are typically territorial, exploiting the food in their own area and defending it against intruders of their own species. Quite a small area may support a pair of birds all year round, but only if the owners of the territory can enjoy more or less exclusive possession and can get to know all the resources of the area intimately. Fruit-eating birds, on the other hand, cannot live in this way; a territory small enough to be defended cannot be counted on to provide a continuous food supply. But wherever the fruit is found it tends to be very abundant; often, in fact, so abundant that the fruit-eaters cannot eat it all. Defending such a source of food against intruders, even if it were possible, would be an unnecessary waste of energy. Social feeding in fact is a positive advantage, since with many individuals on the lookout for food each tree is likely to be quickly located as its fruit ripens.

This difference in social organization between insectivores and frugivores—on the one hand a territorial system in which evenly distributed but not very abundant food resources are partitioned, and on the other hand a system of communal exploitation of a spatially unstable but abundant food supply —is perhaps the most obvious of the consequences of choosing either insects or fruit as a basic diet. But for some birds there has been another equally important consequence. This depends on the fact that insects are generally hard to find, so that an insect-eater needs to spend much time in foraging, whereas fruits tend to be abundant and as many as can be eaten can be collected in a short time. Hence insectivorous birds cannot devote a large part of their day to other activities, and both sexes are likely to be needed to feed the young. In contrast, frugivorous birds have much time to spare, and it is more likely that one parent alone can feed the young. We found, for example, by maintaining a continuous watch throughout the daylight hours, that a male Bearded Bellbird spent 87 percent of the entire time within his small calling area, and a male Black-and-white Manakin spent 90 percent of the daylight hours at his court.

These are preconditions that must have made possible the evolution of the elaborate courtship displays of the cotingas and manakins. Once the male is able to devote a great deal of his time to activities other than foraging, and in addition is no longer needed at the nest, he is free to mate with as many females as he can attract. Under these circumstances males become intense sexual rivals; the ability to attract females is all-important, and the most elaborate adornments and displays will be favored by natural selection if they serve this end. Sexual profligacy, not the patient care of a family, is the way in which the male is likely to be able to contribute most to future generations. The old naturalists who liked to draw morals from nature would have found the cotingas awkward subjects.

Not all fruit-eating birds are specialists, however; only a few have gone the way of the cotingas and manakins. I have made a comparison between the two extremes, but many forest birds, in fact probably the majority, eat both insects and fruit. Even the manakins occasionally take insects, and they regularly feed insects as well as fruit to their young. The whole thing is of course vastly complicated, but one thing at least seems certain and is of fundamental importance: the evolution of the fruit-eating birds and of the fruits that they eat has been a mutual process; each has affected the other. It has been a very different process from the interaction of birds and the insects that they feed on.

The fruit offers the bird something of value, a more or less nutritious flesh surrounding the seed or seeds. The bird in return offers the food plant a service, by removing the seeds and scattering them somewhere where they may grow, well beyond the distance that they could reach unaided. The plant has to devote some of its resources to the seeds—they may be small, with few food reserves, or large with ample reserves—and it has to devote some resources to the part of the fruit that the birds eat, in the form of sugars, fats, and proteins, in order to make it a food worth the bird's taking. The bird, for its part, has to swallow and then regurgitate, or void in its feces, a certain amount of ballast which is of no nutritive value, the seeds; it may have to transport this ballast some distance before it gets rid of it. It is a fascinating exercise to try to see how the bargain has been struck between the various kinds of fruiting trees and the birds that feed at them. One has to speculate freely, since the subject has been much neglected and the facts are hard to come by; but the speculation leads to predictions and one can test one's predictions against new facts as they become available. If the facts fit the predictions, there is some reason to suppose that the speculations are on the right lines.

Trees and shrubs that are adapted to colonize clearings and forest edges tend to produce many small seeds. It is apparently most important that they should have the greatest possible chance of establishing themselves quickly on any piece of open ground that may be available. For obvious reasons, a larger number of small seeds is better for this purpose than a few large seeds, for in any area where there is a rich flora competition between different species for a foothold on any new patch of ground will be intense. Such plants usually produce fruit regularly and prolifically, presumably for the same reason, and this means that they cannot devote a great amount of their limited resources to each fruit. But to attract birds it is sufficient to coat the seeds with a succulent flesh containing energy-giving carbohydrates and little else, and this is what these plants do. In Trinidad the family Melastomaceae is the oustanding example. Their bunches of small, many-seeded fruits, looking rather like elderberries, attract almost every small and medium-sized bird that eats any fruit at all, and melastome seedlings often outnumber those of all other plants combined along forest paths and on open ground suitable for colonization.

Attractive though melastome and similar fruits are to birds of many kinds, they cannot provide a balanced diet. The birds that eat them must also eat insects (or some other food rich in protein). The melastome type of fruit does not allow the evolution of the most specialized kinds of frugivorous birds, those that eat fruit and nothing else, but it is ideal for the more generalized bird that will readily exploit a fruit supply while it lasts and then will turn to other sources of food. The tanagers are the prime example of such birds in the New World tropics, but thrushes, flycatchers, vireos, even woodpeckers, and many others are all to be seen at the melastome feast.

For trees of primary, or undisturbed, forest the problem of dispersal is very different. Only rarely does a new tree get a chance to establish itself and grow to full size. Seedlings must begin to grow in the deep shade of the forest floor, and must then wait for more space and more light before they can make further progress. It must be an advantage for such trees to have large seeds provided with ample food reserves. Of course there is a tremendous range of seed types, but on average the seeds of the true forest trees are a good deal larger than the seeds of trees of secondary vegetation. The forest tree's strategy is to produce fewer seeds and give each one a better chance to survive, rather than a large number of seeds each of which has a very poor chance.

It is very puzzling how the seeds of some forest trees are dispersed. Some produce huge heavy fruits that fall beneath the tree, or at most are shifted a few yards by some animal. But for a large number of forest trees there is no problem: they are clearly adapted for dispersal by birds. Their fruits are varied in type, as one would expect; but there is one rather common type, a fruit like an olive or small hard plum, with a single rather large seed surrounded by a firm but often thin layer of flesh. The fruit is simple in structure, but it is the product of a subtle bargain struck between tree and bird, a compromise in which the advantages and disadvantages are nicely balanced.

From the point of view of the tree, the problem is to coat the large seed with a flesh attractive enough and of a suitable size to be sought after by birds, without expending too much of its resources on the coating. A thick succulent flesh containing mainly carbohydrates and water might be a possible solution, but such a fruit would have to be very large to be worth taking, ballast and all. It would be too large for most birds, and they would be more likely to pick off the flesh rather than to remove the whole fruit. This is evidently not a very good strategy for a forest tree, and few kinds have adopted it. The more usual strategy is to coat the large seed with a rather dry and very nutritious flesh, so that the whole thing is not too bulky. If the flesh is nutritious enough it will be well worth eating, even though a large fraction of the fruit may be useless ballast. Having swallowed it, it will be to the bird's advantage to get rid of the seed fairly quickly, so that more fruits can be accommodated.

For the bird, an important consequence follows. The flesh of such a fruit is now nutritious enough to be a complete diet in itself; even the nestlings can be reared on such fruit.[23] The way is open for the final stage in the increasing inter-dependence of bird and food tree. The birds become wholly dependent on the fruit for the essential nutriments (they may also feed on occasion on less nutritious fruits). The trees in their turn become dependent for effective dispersal of their seeds on a smaller number of dispersal agents than the trees and shrubs with smaller fruits and less nutritious fruits; but their agents of dispersal are more reliable, since they are themselves dependent on the trees.

The very nutritious fruits do not need to advertise themselves in the same way as the fruits of trees and shrubs that attract the less specialized, more opportunistic fruit-eaters. They are often quite-dull-colored, blackish or dull purple or even green. The specialized fruit-eating birds know the food trees in their area well, returning to them day after day, while the fruit lasts, and year after year. Nor are the fruits obviously very palatable. They tend to be dry and often bitter, and naturalists have commented with surprise on how unattractive they seem to be; but these unattractive qualities are the consequences of their being suitable as a staple diet. We could survive longer on olives than on red currants and raspberries.

The bargain struck between the specialized fruit-eater and its food trees is not difficult to understand in simple outline, but there are still some challenging problems. If the seed itself is large and contains food reserves for the future seedling, it should be as good a food as the fruit's outer flesh or even better. But although there are birds which destroy tree seeds—for example many parrots and some pigeons—the "legitimate" fruit-eaters regurgitate the seeds intact after digesting off the outer flesh. They must do so, if the system is to work. Some seeds certainly have toxic substances in them and this may be a common deterrent, but few analyses have been made of the seeds of forest trees. The palms, one of the most important tree families producing very nutritious fruits, do not have toxic seeds, but the seed coat is very hard and woody and quite resistant to all birds except the larger parrots. The birds, for their part, have a different problem. They have to take in a larger quantity of ballast with their food; and if even only a few of the fruits that they eat have toxic seeds it becomes vital that they should strip or digest off the flesh without crushing or abrading the seed. Furthermore they must regurgitate the seeds fairly quickly, otherwise their stomachs would soon be filled with seeds and the whole method might be uneconomical. The mechanism is not understood, but, not surprisingly, specialized fruit-eating birds do have the ability to regurgitate large seeds clean and intact not long after the fruit has been swallowed. Most of our studies of the food of the cotingas and manakins were based on collecting and identifying the seeds which they constantly regurgitate while they are on their display perches or their nests.

Only a few tree families and a few bird families have taken this evolutionary course and made a mutual bargain—reliable dispersal of seed in exchange for a complete and sufficient food supply. It has been a long process, molding the evolution of both fruit and bird. In the New World tropics the most important of the tree families involved are the laurels (Lauraceae), the palms (Palmae), the incense family (Burseraceae), and the ivy family (Araliaceae), with the nutmegs (Myristicaceae), myrtles (Myrtaceae), and a few others of secondary importance. Of the bird families, the cotingas are certainly the most important; there can be little doubt that the evolution of the larger cotingas has been intimately bound up with the evolution of trees of the above-named families.

Yet once more, O ye laurels, and once more
Ye myrtles brown, with ivy never sear,
I come to pluck your berries harsh and crude . . .

Milton might have been putting words into the mouth of a foraging bellbird.

The laurels are one of the most difficult families of trees for the forest botanist; there are very many species and they are confusingly similar to one another. We sometimes wished that we had easier trees to identify when we were trying to catalogue the diet of our birds; but we eventually realized that it was not a question of bad luck. Almost certainly, it is because they are adapted for dispersal by the cotingas and other birds of about the same size that the laurels are so uniform in fruit structure. The melastomes show a similar proliferation of similar-looking species, and the explanation is probably the same. For the botanist in the herbarium the problem is especially acute. In life each species has its own characteristics. The color of the undersides of the leaves and of dead and dying leaves; the way the leaves hang; the color and texture of the bark; the color of the bloom on ripe fruit; such things, with a little experience, enable one to pick out each tree at a glance. All these become useless when the specimen is dried and pressed. The botanist in the herbarium may be unable to make his identification without a specimen of the flower, which he has to dissect in order to examine the minute floral structures on which the diagnosis of the species was based.[24]

If a large number of trees, all rather similar to one another and all with fruit whose seeds are dispersed by birds, are growing together in the same area of forest, competition may be a problem for them. They may each have slightly different requirements of soil, terrain, drainage, and slope, so that all can coexist as mature trees in the same area, but even so they will be competitors for their agents of dispersal. Imagine that all flowered and fruited at about the same time of year. There would be an enormous abundance of fruit for a limited period each year; probably more fruit would be available at that time than the fruit-eaters could consume, and competition between the trees would be intense. Any tree that began to alter its fruiting season would have a great advantage; it might then be the only tree providing fruits at the time and all fruit-eaters would flock to it.

In temperate latitudes the seasons are so marked that flowering and fruiting seasons have only limited scope for alteration. But in the humid tropics the physical environment may allow a tree to flower and fruit at any time, and so the advantage of fruiting at a different time from trees of other species may be an important factor in the evolution of flowering and fruiting seasons. Much more field work will have to be done before we can tell how important this process has been; but for the Trinidad melastomes at least it seems the most likely explanation of their seasons. In the Arima Valley there are at least twenty more or less common species of melastomes in the genus *Miconia*, and between them they provide food throughout the year. Since all of them grow within a few square miles and one may find several species within a few yards of one another, it is difficult to believe that their fruiting seasons can be adapted to their physical environments. But the advantage of avoiding competition for the limited number of dispersal agents by not all fruiting at the same time is obvious.

This leads to the last, and perhaps the most important, of the consequences of eating fruit. If the food trees, as a result of competition among themselves for their dispersal agents, are forced to stagger their fruiting seasons throughout the year, the birds have in effect ensured for themselves a continuous food supply. Fruit-eating birds of tropical forests thus not only propagate their food trees by dispersing the seed but they also, it seems, create for themselves a reliable succession of fruits throughout the year. I do not know of any other case of an animal so successfully ensuring its own food supply.

6

Sexual Selection

This will be an unsatisfactory chapter, discussing interesting theoretical questions but doing so inconclusively for lack of the critical evidence. The main question is easy to formulate: what is the evolutionary process that has led to the development of the exuberant male adornments and elaborate displays which we have been describing? The predisposing conditions seem fairly clear; they were dealt with in the last chapter. As far as the cotingas and manakins are concerned, and putting it at its simplest, the whole thing seems to be a consequence of eating fruit in tropical forest, a way of life that leaves adult birds with much spare time and makes it possible for the female to attend the nest single-handed. But to identify the predisposing factors is not to explain the process to which they give rise.

As in many lines of evolutionary inquiry, the problem was first clearly seen, and a reasonable solution proposed, by Charles Darwin. Darwin distinguished two kinds of selection which, according to his theory, act on the inheritable differences between individuals and result in what he called descent with modification and we now usually call evolution. By far the more important was "natural selection," the process which favors those individuals which are "fittest," or best adapted to survive in the struggle for existence. The other was "sexual selection," a process which in Darwin's words "depends on the advantage which certain individuals have over others of the same sex and species solely in respect of reproduction." A chapter in *The Origin of Species* was devoted to sexual selection, and much fuller treatment was given to it in *The Descent of Man,* published ten years later in 1869.

Darwin ascribed to sexual selection all those male characters which are used in obtaining a mate, whether by courtship or by direct struggle between rival males, and which may be so extravagantly developed that one would suppose they actually lower the possessor's general "fitness." There are obviously two different kinds of characters which should be subject to sexual selection: on the one hand, such things as the antlers of male deer, by means of which a stag can hold a harem of females against his rivals; and on the other hand, such things as the Peacock's train or the male Cock-of-the rock's plumage, which are used to attract and impress the female and not, so far as known, to deter rival males. Rather different considerations apply to these two kinds of character, and we shall be concerned only with the latter, and only with their development in birds, since birds are the subject of this book and Darwin too devoted more space to them than to any other group of animals.

Darwin's theory seems very reasonable, and with some modification it has stood the test of time. He applied it rather too widely, however, and a good many of his examples have had to be pruned away. In particular, he used it to explain differences between the sexes which we can now see have other causes than the advantage which they may give to one individual over another "solely in respect of reproduction"— unless, of course, one interprets reproduction in the widest sense to mean not just securing a mate but contributing offspring to future generations, in which case no distinction can be drawn between sexual selection and natural selection.

Because of these and other shortcomings the theory was strongly criticized, and many zoologists rejected it completely. Some far more unlikely theories were, in fact, proposed in its place, such as that male adornments were somehow the spontaneous outcome of surplus vitality.[25] But as more and more observations were made on courtship behavior it became clear that males which have striking adornments adopt exactly those postures and movements which show them off to the female to best advantage. Another crucial fact became apparent, that extravagant characters used in courtship are mainly to be found in species in which the male's contribution to reproduction ends when he has succeeded in mating. The cotingas and manakins are good examples, and Darwin mentioned some of them in *The Descent of Man*, though all he had to go on was their skins and, in the case of the Cock-of-the-rock, a quite inaccurate account of courtship behavior. He did not know that the male is emancipated from nesting duties, nor did he mention their feeding habits which, as I have argued earlier, allow the males to spend most of their time in display and the females to attend the nest single-handed.

Much depends on this complete separation of the roles of the sexes. It must be to the male's advantage to fertilize as many females as possible, so that adornments which are positively harmful in other ways may be favored by selection as long as they are effective in courtship. The female on the other hand stakes all her resources on raising her family single-handed; she has plenty of opportunity to select a mate, and if by selecting the best mate she can enhance her offspring's chances of survival she will gain greatly thereby. In selecting a mate she has everything to gain by being discriminating, while the male has nothing to lose, and everything to gain, by being profligate and undiscriminating.

Darwin's main argument, at least as it applies to birds like cotingas, birds of paradise, and Peacocks, seems unanswerable. Nevertheless some real difficulties remain. One of these is the question of female choice. Obviously, the extravagant male characters (including their behavior), which we are trying to account for, have been developed over long periods of time, probably to be measured in hundreds of thousands of years. There must have been some process of selection which resulted in the building up of the extraordinarily complex hereditary basis for the characters we see today; those individual males in which they were best developed *must* have had an advantage over the others. What, other than the females, could have been the selecting agent? Darwin accepted the logical necessity, as it appears, that the female "by a long selection of the more attractive males added to their beauty or other attractive qualities." He went on: "No doubt this implies powers of discrimination and taste on the part of the female which will at first appear extremely improbable; but by the facts to be adduced hereafter, I hope to be able to show that the females actually have these powers."

Critics pointed out that there was no evidence for a sense of "beauty" in the female, as the theory demanded. If they have no appreciation of beauty why should the male characters which they are supposed to have preferred seem beautiful to us? This does not now seem a fatal objection. It is only necessary that we should perceive beauty in what the female bird need only see as "striking"; and we have an infinite capacity for seeing beauty in objects and appearances which, at least as far as scientific explanation is concerned, were obviously not designed to be beautiful to us—for instance a sunset, a butterfly, or a microscopic organism.

But the criticism does probe a weak spot in Darwin's argument, though not very effectively. In spite of the facts which he adduced, Darwin had no real evidence that females prefer to mate with those males that are best endowed with the trappings used in courtship. He knew that birds have senses acute enough to perceive small differences, and that females under conditions of captivity often show a very definite preference for one male over others. He knew also that in natural conditions it is a general rule that males establish territories and advertise themselves in some way, and that females visit them in their territories, so that there is plenty of opportunity for the females to exercise a choice. The circumstantial evidence is very strong. Nevertheless there was no critical evidence in Darwin's day, and as far as I know there is none today, except for one rather atypical case, that in species in which display and the associated adornments are highly developed the females prefer the best-endowed males.

One might suppose that such evidence should most easily be found in birds that display in leks, where the females (and the human observer) can see and compare many different males. When I was studying the Black-and-white Manakin in Trinidad I paid some attention to this point. I could detect no difference, however, in performance between males; but some males were much more successful than others in attracting females, and what clearly was important was the position of the court. The holders of central courts were the most successful in attracting females, and their courts were the most coveted by other males. After I left Trinidad, Dr. Alan Lill spent four years studying the Golden-headed Manakin and Black-and-white Manakin with the express aim of analyzing the displays and mating success of individual males.[26] Again, he could find no individual differences in *performance* which he could correlate with mating success, but birds with a more central position in the leks were on average the most successful.

There are some possible ways out of this difficulty. Whatever the males' position at the display ground may be, there might be exceedingly slight differences in appearance and display behavior between males, which would need the most refined techniques of measurement, based on cine-photography and sound recording, for us to detect, and the females may distinguish between males on this basis, preferring some to others. The success of each individual male might thus depend on small differences in his adornments and his ability to display them, as well as on the position of his court. When one considers that chicks of colonial seabirds can distinguish the calls of their parents among the hubbub of hundreds of others, and that many birds are known to be able to recognize their mates, parents, or neighbors by their appearance, even at a considerable distance, it does not seem impossible that females should react to differences in the displays of different males that are too slight for us to detect. The one atypical case which I mentioned above is relevant here. The Ruff is one of a small number of northern wading birds in which the males display in leks on open meadow and marshland, much as manakins do in tropical forests. In one respect it is unique, for as is well known the males are by no means alike but differ most strikingly in their ornamental head plumage. The Ruff is also of all lek birds the most accessible to European ornithologists and it has been very well studied, especially in the Netherlands, where it has been found that the males whose plumes are best developed and most striking to the human observer are also the most successful in obtaining mates.[27] The reason why the males vary so much is problematical, but the important point for the present purpose is that in the one bird in which we can see that there are individual differences between males we know that the females are influenced in their choice by these differences.

Another explanation that has been put forward is that the vigor and aggressiveness which enable a male to obtain a favorable territory for his display—a central court, in the case of the manakins—are linked genetically to the sexual characters which we are trying to account for. To put it more generally, the best adorned male may also be the most vigorous, so that even if the females do not actively select the best adorned the result will be the same as if they did. This suggestion cannot be disproved, but it is not very convincing. In the first place we may note that such a process would not be sexual selection in the proper sense, for the best endowed males would presumably be at a general advantage over other males by virtue of their greater vigor, not merely at an advantage "solely in respect of reproduction." But in any case, such an explanation does not account for the fact that the adornments of males are so clearly "designed" to be visually striking—some, in fact, such as the eyes in the Peacock's train, far more so than anything that the cotingas and manakins can display. Why, in fact, if the male's vigor were all that is important, need it be linked with any adornment at all? We are on much stronger ground if we stick to the original idea that the females do actively select the males on the basis of their individual adornments and performance, even if we cannot prove that they do so.

It may be noted in passing that if it is hard to get evidence for selection of males by females in a lek species, where both the females and the human observer can see and compare several males at the same time, it is difficult even to imagine how the females exercise selection in birds like pheasants and some birds of paradise, in which the males display in isolated territories. As Derek Goodwin has remarked to me, the hen Golden Pheasant must be imagined saying to herself, as she gazes at the gorgeous plumage of a displaying cock, something like: "He's not so good as the male I visited ten minutes ago. Let's see if the male in the next clearing is any better." It strains one's imagination; but so do a lot of things in nature which are nevertheless true.

Another puzzling fact, which one encounters again and again, is that whenever a species with well-developed male plumage and adornments is split into isolated populations, each separate population tends to evolve along its own line, differentiating in ways that seem quite arbitrary. Other species evolve minor differences when they are broken into separate populations, but these usually involve only slight changes in general color, size, proportions, etc., and such differences on closer examination can usually be seen to be related to the different climates and other environmental influences to which the different populations are exposed. But the differences which evolve in isolated populations of the kind of bird we are discussing have no such basis. Why, for instance, in one isolated population of bellbirds should the males develop three long bare wattles from the base of the beak, in another population a single wattle studded with small feathers, in another a beard consisting of a mass of stringy wattles on the throat, and in another a bare throat of colored skin? Why, in one of the four groups into which the blue-backed manakin stock was split, should the males have developed long central tail feathers projecting like filaments four inches beyond the others, while in another the tail remained normal, and in another the central pair of feathers became about an inch longer than the rest?

Examples could be multiplied by about as many times as there are groups of related species. One cannot avoid the conclusion that in such species some very powerful but arbitrary selective force is continually working on the males, and that it is only the genetic connection between members of more or less continuous populations—what is usually called "gene flow"—that keeps each species more or less uniform throughout its range.

In some animals, the appearance of the males and their elaborate courtship displays are known to act as "isolating mechanisms"—they are one of the means by which closely related species avoid hybridizing with each other. The females have an innate recognition of the right male by his appearance and behavior, and they certainly exercise a choice, but the choice is between males of the right species and males of other species. At the same time they must tend to select from among the males of their own species those that conform to their innately recognized pattern and reject any that deviate from it. This process is probably important in many cases where several closely related species of animals occur together in the same area; but it does not account for the apparently arbitrary evolution of male adornments which we are discussing. All the evidence shows that the bellbirds, for example, have evolved by the splitting of one ancestral form, followed by the further evolution of the daughter populations in isolation from one another. It seems almost certain that when each of them was developing its characteristic ornamentation it was not in contact with any other bellbird, or with any other species at all like a bellbird. Exactly the same goes for the Cock-of-the-rock, the Umbrella-bird, and several other cotingas, and there is no case for which a convincing explanation can be based on the idea that the differences between species have resulted from the need to avoid hybridization.

If there has been no need for the female to discriminate between the "right" males (those that are of her species) and the "wrong" males, has she in fact any innate preference for the adornments and displays of the males of her own species? May she not be attracted by any striking display? The answer is not known. It would have to be based on experimentation, which would be feasible in small birds like manakins if they were kept in aviaries large enough for their normal behavior to be shown, but would be difficult for the larger cotingas. If there is no strong innate preference, there would be nothing to check or guide the further evolution of male adornments in any isolated population. Whatever might be the extravagances of males, in appearance or behavior, the females might simply prefer those that were the most extravagant. We still would not know what causes the males to evolve in the seemingly arbitrary ways that they do.

The whole subject bristles with problems and provokes questions which cannot be answered. Another important one has not yet been touched on at all: why should the males of some species gather in leks? If a male displayed on his own in the forest—and in many species the males do display alone—surely he would attract females and would mate with some. Would it not be better, for example, for a male Black-and-white Manakin to set up a display area on his own, instead of establishing himself at an outlying court at a lek, with little prospect of mating until he can obtain one of the more favored central courts? I think that the answer must be that a group of males is so much more effective at attracting females than a single male would be that it is on average an advantage to a member of a group. It is obviously an overwhelming advantage for a bird that occupies a central position in the group, while the outlying and relatively unsuccessful members have a chance of eventually taking over a central court. There are two reasons why a group will attract very many more females than a single bird. First, the group is permanent, while even the most persistent single bird cannot be displaying all the time. Once a female has learned where the group is she can go straight there with the certainty of finding males ready to mate with her. Secondly, the combined effect of the displays of many males is much more arresting than anything that a single male can manage. The human observer finds it stimulating, and there is every reason to suppose that a bird finds it even more so.

A group of males can enhance their individual effects by displaying close together, each as a unit. But they can do so in another way, by combining to give a joint performance. Why only the blue-backed manakins have done this is another of the many questions which cannot be answered. Their system is a very different one from that of the more typical lek birds. The group of males is smaller, and within it the dominant male probably does all the mating and the subordinate birds none. A subordinate bird cannot advertise himself effectively except with a dominant one; he has no alternative but to wait in the hope of becoming the dominant bird himself. And the dominant bird too sacrifices some of his independence, since no single bird is an effective unit in the business of attracting and holding the female in the first stages of courtship. When we find birds pooling their resources like this, and apparently losing some of their independence as individuals, we begin to suspect that some sort of "kin selection" may be operating—in other words, that the members of a group may be more closely related to one another than to individuals in other groups, so that the dominance of the individual who is successful in mating, and the subordinate behavior of the individuals who fill the supporting roles, are both positively advantageous forms of behavior promoting the success of the group. But nothing is yet known of the composition or family relationships of groups of blue-backed or of any other species of manakins.

There is another possibility. If a group of males is so small that it can be effectively dominated by one bird, so that he is the only one that regularly mates with visiting females— and this seems to be the case in the blue-backed manakins— then it may be an advantage for the subordinate males to assist the dominant male in advertising the display area, whether they are related to him or not. A subordinate male's best chance of mating will depend on his eventually becoming the dominant bird; if, as a subordinate, he has helped to advertise the display area and make it more attractive to females he may later reap his reward. This may be an especially sound strategy for a young male if an individual's expectation of life is very high (as we know it is in at least one species of manakin), so that senility becomes a common contributory cause of death. For in such a population a young bird is likely to outlive an older bird, and so may take over its position. In many birds of higher latitudes annual death rates are very high and are independent of age, so that a young bird is no more likely to outlive an older one than vice versa. If this argument is sound, the blue-backed manakins' strategy could evolve only in the equable conditions of the tropical forest.

7

The Calfbird

When we went to southern Guyana for three months in 1970 and camped in the forest at the foot of the Kanuku Mountains, Barbara's main objective was to make a fuller study of the Calfbird, which she had briefly watched ten years earlier in the same area. What she had seen then had shown that this large and grotesque cotinga is as remarkable in its behavior as it is in appearance and voice; but much remained unknown. In her application to the Frank Chapman Memorial Fund of the American Museum of Natural History, which gave her a generous grant toward the expenses of the 1970 trip, she said that she intended, among other things, to discover the Calfbird's nest, which had never been found—a bold declaration of intent when one considers how difficult it usually is to find almost any kind of a nest in tropical forests, that some species have been studied over periods of years without their nests being discovered, and that the Calfbird is not an abundant bird.

Then, on the day before our departure, in the middle of the last hectic stages of packing, she tripped coming down our narrow stairs, fell the last few steps, and broke her ankle. The whole expedition should perhaps have been abandoned, or at least postponed; but she decided to push on. The details of the next four or five days are not relevant to Calfbirds, but the outcome was that Barbara arrived at the clearing in the forest where we were to camp, hobbling on a crutch and with one leg in plaster. For the first two weeks she could not move far along the rough trails which led up the valley. But her ankle mended well; the plaster, soaked by rain and mud, disintegrated rather rapidly, and I finally hacked the last pieces of it off with a penknife a few days before the date the doctor had prescribed. Meanwhile, Barbara had been able to hobble far enough to begin a most effective study of Calfbirds, a group of which had their headquarters about half a mile from the camp; and she ended by finding three occupied nests, all within a mile of the camp.[28] A more mobile observer might very easily have dissipated his energies searching further afield and have found nothing.

Calfbirds are the buffoons of the cotinga family. Their appearance is faintly ludicrous, their voices absurdly unbird-like, they indulge in horseplay, and they break many of the rules and spoil the neat generalizations which one laboriously tries to formulate. They are altogether "singular and un-matched," and serve as a healthy warning against putting too much reliance on one's oversimplified evolutionary explana-tions, which may be sound enough as far as they go but only account for a fraction of the facts. For these reasons I have put this chapter after the last two chapters of discussion and generalization; one needs to have an idea of the rules in order to appreciate how the Calfbird breaks them.

It is a stocky bird about the size of a small crow, with a short tail, powerful legs, and a heavy crowlike beak made more prominent by the fact that the forepart of the head is completely bare except for some sparse hairlike bristles. The bare skin of the head is gray blue. The plumage is mainly umber brown, grading to a brighter and more cinnamon shade on the underparts; wings and tail are blackish. The baldness of the crown is made more striking by the thick plumage of the back of the head, which stands up in the form of a monk's hood or cowl. The sexes are alike except that the males are a little larger than females.

Most of the early travelers in Guyana remarked on the voice of the Calfbird, which gives it its name. "Then, also in the forest," wrote im Thurm in his most interesting book *Among the Indians of Guiana* (1883), "is heard an extraordinarily deep sound, like the lowing of an ox, and it is long before the traveller realizes the fact that this is made by the 'quow' or 'calf-bird.' " "The Bare-headed Chatterer or Quow-birds (*Gymnocephalus calvus*) bellowed, with a sound as though from a herd of oxen grazing in the forest," wrote J. J. Quelch in *Timehri* (1883). Indeed, no other significant fact appears to have been recorded on the Calfbird, for the usual reason: that if the traveler deviated from his path to get closer to a calling Calfbird, it was in order to shoot it, after which nothing of any further interest could be observed.

When we first went to Guyana in 1960 and found a place where Calfbirds were calling, Barbara sat down to watch them, and she soon found that a group of birds were in the habit of coming together to call in a small area of forest, where they occupied a number of favored perches at no great height, well below the forest canopy. It seemed to be a kind of group display in which the strange call, accompanied by equally strange postures, served as the chief means of advertisement. But time was too short on that occasion to work out the roles of the different individuals at the display ground.

Jan Lindblad had made tape recordings of the calls of Calf-birds not far from his camp in the Kanuku Mountains in 1969, so we knew that we had a good chance of finding them when we decided to use his old campsite the following year. Soon after we arrived, while Barbara was still unable to walk far, I asked William, our Amerindian helper, to show me where the birds had been calling the year before. In fact we would have found them easily in any case, as the place was barely half a mile up the valley and the sound of the calling could be heard from the main trail. As soon as she was mobile enough Barbara went there, and from then on she spent a few hours there nearly every day, simply sitting on the ground, in a position from which she could see the birds on their perches thirty or forty feet overhead. All that was necessary was to cut a few saplings and shrubs that obscured the view. To collect the seeds regurgitated by the Calfbirds, she cleared the ground below their perches of fallen leaves and other debris, and thus got a very complete record of their food during the three months of observation. The Calf-birds were rather shy at first, probably because the local people sometimes shot at them, but they soon became used to her presence and did not bother to leave their perches when she arrived.

For most of our stay the weather was dry; mosquitoes and other annoying insects were practically absent. It was a wonderfully rich area of forest and when the Calfbirds were inactive there were plenty of other things to watch. A pair of great Black Curassows, game birds the size of small turkeys, regularly foraged on the ground beneath the Calfbirds, walk-ing quietly about unaware that they were being watched, the male keeping contact with his mate by uttering at regular intervals a very low-pitched "oomper OOMP"; and once, as Barbara sat very still in her usual spot, an Amerindian came creeping along with his bow drawn, intent on stalking the curassows, until to his amazement he almost stumbled upon her. Often a troupe of monkeys passed through the trees overhead, and once a Tayra, a heavily built member of the weasel family, trotted within a few feet of her. While she watched, a passing Cock-of-the-rock came and peered down at the patch of bare earth below one of the Calfbirds' perches, evidently puzzled to find what appeared to be a new "court" on the forest floor in a place a long way from any Cock-of-the-rock display ground. Once she saw a White Bellbird picking twigs from a tree that happened to be in view—very fine twigs almost certainly used for its nest lining. We never found the White Bellbird's nest—nobody has ever found it—but the same tree was visited by a Purple-throated Fruit-crow, and by telling me which way it flew off she put me on the track of its nest which I eventually found about two hundred yards away. Many of our most exciting chance encounters have come in this way, simply by sitting still, and not a few of them have been of real significance for some quite different line of research. The forest is full of things to be discovered, and mostly they are to be found not by actively searching, but by passively waiting and watching.

In making sense of her observations, Barbara's most serious difficulty was to distinguish between the individuals and to know their sexes. There were four birds with established, regularly occupied perches at the display ground, and four birds which were present morning and evening but absent for long periods in the day. These latter four came into a good deal of conflict with each other and with the established owners. All eight birds regularly mooed; but the calls of the four unestablished birds were less perfectly developed than those of the other four. One of the unestablished birds had a most unusual moo, about an octave higher than normal. He was christened "falsetto," and in addition to being readily identifiable at the display ground the occasional moos which he made while he was away feeding greatly helped to define the area of forest over which the group ranged. The other three unestablished birds had slight differences in the quality and duration of their moos, which were probably signs of varying degrees of immaturity.

It seemed fairly certain that these eight birds were males, but only measurement of a bird in the hand could settle the question. After a few weeks' watching Barbara decided to try to trap some of the birds. If the attempt were successful, she would not only gain information on their sex but would have some individually marked birds to watch and the whole study would become easier. At the same time she did not want to disturb the birds unduly, as they had lost their shyness; so the operation had to be brief.

We could not possibly have managed it without help. We had nets, but it was necessary to set them at a height of about thirty feet, where there was little to attach them to except the smooth, vertical, and ant-infested trunks of the smaller trees. As so often happens in such circumstances, we relied entirely upon the physical abilities of the local people to do what we would have been utterly unable to do ourselves. William and a friend swarmed up strategically placed trees and managed to string two nets in what we hoped would be the flight paths of the Calfbirds as they approached or left their perches. We then left the nests and waited. Two or three birds of other species got entangled and a good deal of time was wasted while William and his friend climbed the trees, lowered the nets, and extracted them. By the end of the second day we had achieved a limited success. One Calfbird was caught; another went into the net but most unfortunately managed to escape just as William was about to get it out. The bird that was caught was an undoubted male from its measurements; and later observation showed that it was one of the two dominant birds of the group. If only one bird was to be caught, it was a good one to catch. It confirmed what was by now nearly a certainty, that the birds which were regularly present at the display ground were males.

The immediate sequel to the catching and ringing of this bird was interesting. It must have been a traumatic experience; he was caught in a net, extracted and put in a bag, taken half a mile to camp, and there measured, weighed, ringed, and photographed before being released. On the following morning he was back on his perch but evidently still feeling the aftereffects, as he periodically closed his eyes and sank back on his tarsi, as if to sleep. By the following morning he had been driven from his perch by his immediate neighbor, who had previously been subordinate to him. There had evidently been a fight, as there were forty-two Calfbird body feathers lying below the perch which had not been there the day before. For seven days the rival male remained in possession of the perch, while the owner, now identifiable by his white ring, spent most of his time on the periphery of the display ground. Then, during a period of high activity at the display ground, during which a female was visiting the males, the ringed bird regained his perch and he remained in possession for the rest of our stay. The incident demonstrated more clearly than anything else could that the males are in constant rivalry, and that those in possession of the favored perches need to assert themselves constantly in order to maintain their position.

Occasionally other birds visited the display ground, and

behaved quite differently from the birds in regular occupation. They were silent and usually remained in the trees above the display perches, to which they occasionally flew down. Once one of these birds was briefly mounted by the owner of the display perch. These visiting birds were presumed to be females, and in one case the presumption was practically a certainty. The displaced male regained his perch, as mentioned above, during a period of high activity when a presumed female was visiting the display ground. This was five or six days before an egg was laid in one of the nests nearby, and so coincided exactly with the period when the egg must have been fertilized.

I have gone to some length in dealing with the identity and sex of the birds at the display ground, but even so have left out a good deal of detail and have given only the main conclusion. In fact, very careful and prolonged observation was needed to establish the number of males and their mutual relationships; but in the course of this observation Barbara at the same time saw the full range of the remarkable displays with which the birds asserted and maintained their positions. The layout of the display ground and the displays can now be described in more detail.

The display perches were concentrated on a group of six trees spaced each about ten yards apart, the whole area measuring about twenty by thirty yards. The perches were thirty to forty feet up, near the tops of these trees and far below the main forest canopy a hundred feet or so above. Nearly all the trees were of one species; they were slender trees with very fine terminal twigs and foliage, rather like a birch and very different from the large-leaved trees which predominate in the tropical forest. What seemed to be most important for the Calfbirds was that they had about thirty feet of branchless trunk and then a sparse crown of more or less horizontal branches, of which the longest and most horizontal parts served as the display perches. The thin foliage meant that there was a clear outlook from all sides. This species of tree, incidentally, proved to be important in another way. Its fine terminal twigs were used, apparently exclusively, for nest lining by the Purple-throated Fruit-crow, a cotinga which I was studying, probably also by the White Bellbird—one was seen picking the twigs, as already mentioned—and, as it turned out later, by the Calfbirds themselves. We collected specimens of the tree and they were identified as a species of *Eugenia* (Myrtaceae) but this genus is so large, containing so many little known species, that specific identification has not yet been possible.

The moo, with which male Calfbirds advertise their presence at the display ground, is a more complex call than its name suggests, and is accompanied by strange actions. It is as astonishing to watch as it is to hear. First the bird leans slightly forward on its perch and utters a growling "grrr," during which it inhales air. Then it pivots back to an upright position, at the same time raises itself by straightening the flexed leg joint, and utters a louder "aaaa." As it does so, the feathers of the anterior half of the body are fluffed out so that the cowl appears greatly enlarged, and—most surprisingly—two glowing orange balls appear at either side of the tail, like a pair of rear lights. These are, in fact, the curled feathers of the under tail-coverts. From this position the bird sinks backwards through an angle of about twenty degrees, uttering as it does so the loudest part of the call, the lowing "ooooo," which is the only part of the call audible if the bird is heard from a distance. At the same time the tail is depressed so that the under tail-coverts curve round onto the upper surface of the tail. In this position the rear lights glow even more brightly against the black of the tail. This terminal position of the call is most striking: the bird leans back about fifteen degrees from the vertical, all the feathers of the anterior part of the body are raised, and those of the posterior part, except for the tail-coverts, are flattened.

Looking at a museum specimen of a Calfbird one could never guess that the under tail-coverts, which are only a little brighter than the belly plumage and curled, but not otherwise modified, could be put to such effect. The hollow balls of curled feathers appear to catch and transmit the light, and in contrast with the opaque plumage of the rest of the body appear startlingly bright.

Mooing is very much a social activity of male Calfbirds. If

The Calfbird moos; a bird halfway through the call, with body upright and legs fully stretched, and orange "taillights" glowing at either side of the dark tail

only a single bird is present at the display ground he does not moo. He may utter a "half-moo," a version of the call which lacks the final "ooooo," but only when another bird comes within sight or hearing will he give the full moo. When two or more birds are mooing they tend to avoid overlapping their moos. Thus if one bird has begun to moo and another starts just after, the first bird will interrupt his call and wait until the other has finished before beginning again. But although mooing is a social and cooperative activity there is also a constant state of tension between the males which sometimes expresses itself in open aggression. When adult males moo on perches close to one another they usually do so back to back. Sometimes a dominant male would visit one of his neighbors, landing on his display perch and forcing him to retire to the other end of it. Oriented the same way on the perch they would moo alternately, but both would twist their bodies so that they faced as much away from one another as possible.

The four immature males at the display ground mooed more

often than the adults, although the adults were present for a greater portion of the day. There was a strong tendency for a subordinate bird to moo as near to its immediate superior as it could; and when it did so the latter often attacked it. There was something ludicrous in the grotesque bird awkwardly hopping up toward its superior and hopefully mooing, only to be set on and barged off the perch. All the indications were that mooing is a social activity which also acts as a sort of tentative challenge between the mooer and the bird mooed at. It has to be accommodated within a social structure based on constant competition and aggression, overt or latent, between individual males.

Between the adult males, social relationships at the display ground are almost entirely formalized and expressed in displays and postures. I have mentioned how they carefully face away from each other when mooing and avoid overlapping their calls. "Facing away" is a common element in bird behavior and usually signifies appeasement. It is the opposite of the aggressive displaying of the beak, the bird's chief weapon. When an adult male Calfbird is in an aggressive mood it expresses this by adopting a stance that is the very opposite of the mooing posture. All the body feathers are flattened except for the under tail-coverts, which are fluffed out and curve round the tail on either side. The body is held almost horizontally, the tail raised, the wings slightly drooped, and the head and neck are outstretched. Quite motionless, the displaying bird directs its gaze fixedly at its opponent; and to do this it may have to twist its neck somewhat, as it often presents its rear view, with orange taillights at either side of the black tail. Twisting its neck to look back over its shoulder, it manages to combine an aggressive posture with the exhibition of the most striking part of its plumage.

The aggressive posture is assumed very slowly, by imperceptible movements. First the head and neck are stretched forward; then the body plumage is flattened; and finally the horizontal body position is assumed, the tail is raised and the under tail-coverts are fluffed out. The displaying bird may hold the posture for minutes on end, quite motionless. During a two-hour watch on a morning of high activity, when one male was trying to establish itself on a perch near a male that was dominant to it in the hierarchy, the latter was present for the whole time and held the aggressive posture for a total of ninety-three minutes. When the ringed male was temporarily displaced from his perch after the shock of being trapped, he spent long periods in the aggressive posture on the periphery of the display area before he regained his perch.

The immature males at the display ground behaved very differently. They were constantly disputing the possession of perches, and their aggressiveness was seldom expressed in formal displays. Each one frequently displaced the bird immediately below it in the hierarchy, not by adopting formal aggressive postures but simply by flying at it and knocking it off the perch by landing on it, or by hopping along the perch and barging it off. These attacks were often followed by a chase. The aggressiveness persisted when the immature males left the display area on their foraging trips. They were a noisy party, very different from the adult males who were not heard to moo except at the display ground or within a short distance of it. Every now and then the immatures would come close together to moo, and when they did so each bird would usually demonstrate its dominance over its immediate subordinate.

The females also are social. On three occasions Barbara watched two females feeding together, keeping within ten yards of one another, entirely unaggressive and occasionally maintaining contact with subdued calls. On one occasion the two birds were within hearing distance of the display ground. They fed together for twenty minutes; then when the males began mooing the females stopped feeding and flew off towards the display ground. Much more surprisingly, it turned out that these two females nested within a few yards of one another. But before going into this I must return to an earlier stage in the story.

Finding the Calfbird's nest was one of Barbara's main objectives. But it is not easy to know how to go about finding an unknown nest in a tropical forest. Tom Gilliard, on an expedition to eastern Venezuela in 1938, had found a nest in a cave which he thought must have belonged to a Calfbird because it was about the right size and the seeds scattered below it were from fruits eaten by Calfbirds. We were rather doubtful about this, if only because Calfbirds occur in areas where there are no caves. When we asked the local Amerindians in the Kanuku Mountains they said that they nest high up, in holes in trees. This seemed a possibility, as it appeared reasonable that such a large bird might need a very solid support for its nest. On the other hand, the Amerindians said exactly the same when we asked them about the White Bellbird, and we knew this could not be true. It seemed that it might be the standard answer for any largish bird whose nest they did not know. Nevertheless we paid some attention to large trees which looked as if they might have suitable holes, especially if a Calfbird was anywhere near, but without success.

Then on 4 February, only two and a half weeks after we began our observations, Barbara found a nest. She was crouching beside a forest path, watching a flowering vine to see what kinds of hummingbirds might be feeding at it, when she saw a Calfbird with a twig in its beak, only about twenty feet away. The bird evidently had not seen her; it was struggling with the twig, which kept getting caught in the twigs of the small tree in which it was perched. It was a little time before Barbara realized that she was seeing a Calfbird laying the foundations of its nest. The nest was only thirteen feet from the ground; a flimsy basal platform had been laid, at a place where there were several bifurcations near the end of a thin branch.

Eleven days later the nest appeared complete. It was a flattish, loosely knit structure, not unlike a pigeon's nest and surprisingly small for the size of the bird. On a base of coarser twigs the shallow nest cup itself was composed entirely of fine *Eugenia* twigs. Five days after it had been completed, a single egg was laid, pale khaki in ground color and spotted and blotched with brown.

A few days after the egg was laid Barbara had a hide built about ten yards from the nest, a rough structure of palm fronds over a framework of stakes. She spent many hours watching the nest, and I alternated with her in a complete 24-hour watch, from midday on one day to midday on the next. All went well. The female spent long periods on the nest, steadily incubating, occasionally leaving for fairly long periods to feed. Her absences lasted approximately an hour in the early days of incubation and were reduced to about half an hour as incubation advanced. During the 24-hour watch she left the nest only five times.

After twenty-six days of incubation the chick hatched. It was covered with bright orange chestnut down, long and quite thick on the upper surface and sparser below. We continued to watch at the nest, seeing the parent feed it with a variety of large insects, once a small lizard, and occasionally fruit. The day after it hatched, and at weekly intervals after that, we put a rough ladder up to the nest and brought the chick down to examine it. We realized that we were not going to see the end of the nesting cycle. When our time came to leave, nearly nine weeks after the nest had been found, the nestling was eighteen days old and obviously far from fledging. We arranged for William to visit the nest every other day after we had gone, and in due course his report came back to us. The chick was present when twenty-five days old, and had gone two days later; but we suspected that its departure was premature, for when we last saw the chick it did not look as if it could be ready to leave in little more than a week. Even twenty-seven days would be a very short period in comparison with the time taken by other large cotingas.

This nest was about a quarter of a mile from the display ground. The two other nests were even closer, about seventy-five yards from it. Barbara found them simply by keeping a lookout for nests in the same kind of site as the first. In fact they were both not only in the same kind of site but in the same species of tree. From our specimens it was identified for us at Kew as *Rinorea brevipes*, a member of the violet family. It was very common in our area, and it was the tree whose twigs were most favored by the Calfbird for building the base of the nest. Later, continuing to search likely sites, Barbara found two old nests that were almost certainly Calfbirds', probably from the previous year. They too were in similar situations.

What was really surprising about the two new nests was that they were only five yards apart, in adjacent trees. A single egg was laid in each nest, one eight days after the other. Unfortunately they were laid so near the end of our visit that there was no chance of finding out much about them. We built a hide from which both nests could be seen, and Barbara had one three-hour session watching them, just after incubation had begun in the later nest. The two females' sessions on the nest did not coincide—they would hardly have been expected to—but they were evidently associating together to some extent when both were away from their nests, as on one occasion they returned together. The one whose incubation was the more advanced went back onto her nest at once, while the other hung about nearby for a few minutes uttering a low growling call, and then left for another ten minutes' absence.

The simultaneous occupation of two nests so close together raised all sorts of questions, which could not possibly be answered in the time available. One thing seemed fairly certain: that the two nests belonged to the two females which Barbara had watched feeding close to one another and going together to the display ground. But even if female Calfbirds usually associate in couples, is it normal for them to nest close together? One other observation suggested that it may be. When alarmed near the nest, the females utter a rasping "waaaaa." On one occasion when Barbara was watching the first nest from the hide, which was partly open at the back and only well screened on the side facing the nest, a second bird spent over an hour uttering the rasping "waaaaa" from somewhere behind the hide. During some of this time the female that was being watched was on her nest. The significance of the alarm call of a second bird was not apparent until the two adjacent nests were found some time later. We then searched the trees behind the hide, but could find no nest. We could easily have missed one, however, as there were a lot of trees to search and we had no exact idea where to look. Of course it is possible that the two females were a "pair," like the two whose nests were close together, but that only one was nesting at the time and the other was keeping watch and giving the alarm. But it seems more likely that the other one was nesting too, and uttering the alarm call on her own account.

Four days after the egg was laid in the later of the two adjacent nests we packed up camp and left the Kanukus. I regret to say that we ended by robbing the Calfbirds. The third egg, with its nest, came with us, to be added to the collection at the Natural History Museum. The egg white was first carefully extracted and sent in a sealed vial to a specialist in the United States, whose studies of egg white proteins have thrown new light on the relationship between birds. But unfortunately the specimen suffered in transit, and the hope that the Calfbird's egg white might provide a clue to its evolution was not realized.

As we thought about it afterward, we became increasingly impressed by the Calfbird's refusal to be fitted neatly into the theoretical scheme which seems to account quite successfully for many of the main facts about the cotingas, manakins, and other forest birds with lek displays. Here is a species in which groups of males spend most of their time at a traditional display ground, where the females visit them to mate. And yet, if sexual selection is operating—and it should be, just as much as in the Black-and-white Manakin or Cock-of-the-rock—it has produced no difference at all in appearance between the sexes. The slight size difference is much the same as is found in many birds whose habits and ecology are quite different.

Their behavior too is peculiar. In other cotingas and manakins that display in groups, the behavior of the males includes both social and aggressive tendencies, as it does in the Calfbird; but these tendencies are, as it were, overlaid by an elaborate cloak or ritualization. In the Calfbird, both the aggressive and the social tendencies in their behavior seem to be unusually strong. It is a remarkable feature of their group behavior that the most conspicuous of their formalized displays—the moo—seems to be an expression of the social rather than of the aggressive side of their behavior. And another curiosity is that in the most important aggressive display the bird has to face away from its adversary in order to show the "taillights," but this is incompatible with the other main element of the display.

the pointing of the outstretched head and beak at the opponent; with the results that the bird often has to adopt an awkward twisted posture.

Mooing certainly advertises the group of males to interested females. All the males, but especially the subordinate ones, help to make the group conspicuous in this way; but probably only one or two males at the head of the hierarchy have the opportunity to mate. In this the Calfbird is not essentially different from several other cotingas and manakins. What seems peculiar is that, apart from the mooing, the males' behavior appears to be directed almost exclusively toward establishing a strict hierarchy within a small group of individuals. Perhaps there is no question of any choice by the female; she may always mate with the one or two dominant birds. This would at least account for the fact that sexual selection seems not to have operated in the usual way.

In its breeding also the Calfbird breaks some of the rules—or what we think are rules. The great majority of all open nests in tropical forests fail because they are destroyed by predators. This fact has now been abundantly established. Equally well established, I think, is the conclusion that the most important adaptations of nests in the tropical forest are those that help to make them inconspicuous or inaccessible. The Calfbird's nest is a typical example of one of the main inconspicuous types: a small flimsy platform, just big enough to hold the egg and young. In order to be effectively inconspicuous, nests should be spaced far apart. The finding of one nest by a predator must not be an indication that there are others nearby. Conversely, if nests are grouped together they must be inaccessible. These are very general rules; in fact it has often been suggested that one of the important functions of territory in birds is that it spaces nests, so that predation is minimized. Thus the last thing one would expect to find in a tropical forest is two females building easily accessible nests within a few yards of one another.

One has to beware of facile explanations, thought up in order to dispose of awkward facts that do not fit; but a possible one comes to mind. It may be that Calfbirds are large and powerful enough birds to drive off most nest predators, and that two birds nesting close together get an advantage from mutual warning of approaching danger which outweighs the disadvantage that the discovery of one nest may lead to the discovery of the other.

Since the great majority of open nests in the tropical forest fall victim to predators, it must be a great advantage to reduce the time taken for the eggs to hatch and the young to fledge. Because of this, Barbara thought that the Bearded Bellbird's very long fledging period of thirty-five days needed some special explanation, and she suggested that a pure fruit diet might not provide enough protein to allow the chick to grow more quickly. It was most unfortunate that she was not able to get an equally reliable figure for the Calfbird, but when we last examined it the indications were that the nestling was going to take about as long to fledge as the young bellbird. And yet the Calfbird nestling was fed almost entirely on animal food. Again, one looks round for possible explanations. It may be that, if the Calfbird can effectively defend its nest against potential predators, there has not been such strong selection for quick development as in smaller and more defenseless species. We know too little to do more than point out the problem and suggest a plausible answer.

These may all seem trivial problems—except for the bird itself, for which they are all-important. But they are not really trivial, because every detail of an animal's life is relevant to its survival and success, and all of them are interconnected in a complex web of adaptations.

8

Nests

One of the obstacles to the study of tropical forest birds is the difficulty of finding nests. Over a period of ten years Dr. Edwin Willis made a remarkable study of the Ocellated Antbird in Panama, a bird that feeds almost entirely on insects flushed by the marauding columns of army ants on the forest floor. In the course of his work he followed many pairs of color-ringed birds and knew the extent of their territories. He could tell when they were nesting by watching them as they foraged over the ant columns; for instance by the regularly alternating absences of the male and female of a pair when they were incubating their eggs, and later, if their nest was successful, by the appearance of the young birds accompanying their parents. He worked out their very interesting social system in great detail, and has made the Ocellated Antbird one of the best known of tropical forest birds.[29] But he never for certain found an occupied nest, though the nests were certainly within the territories and almost certainly within a few feet of the ground. He suspected that they were placed low down between the buttresses of tree trunks, because he once found a nest with an egg in such a site, which he could attribute to no other bird, and once found an empty nest, and he saw Ocellated Antbirds prospecting such sites.

Of course some nests can be very difficult to find in English woodland, but what can be so frustrating is the difficulty of finding almost *any* nest in tropical forests. There are exceptions: in Trinidad the nests of two forest birds were rather easy to find. One was the Black-and-white Manakin (Chapter 3) and the other the Hairy Hermit, a hummingbird. The nests of two or three others were not very difficult. I think that this was mainly due to the fact that these species were unusually abundant in the area where we worked,[30] and they preferred to nest along streams, which were our main pathways through the forest. On the South American mainland we have never been able to find nests of forest birds in such numbers as we found these, and nobody else has reported doing so.

It is not difficult to see why nests are so hard to find. In tropical forests there are a great many species of birds, but the density of each species is usually low compared with temperate woodland or with nonforest habitats in the tropics. The vegetation is very varied, though it is not usually very dense near ground level; so many different kinds of sites are available. But the main reason is that the nests themselves are so varied, and many of them are hard to see even if one is looking at them.

Nesting in the tropical forests is very difficult. In spite of all precautions a very high percentage of all nests fail, mainly because they fall victim to nest predators, of which there is a greater variety than in any other habitat. In the American tropics the chief nest predators are snakes (of many species), mammals (especially small carnivores and monkeys), and birds (especially toucans). Most of these are visual hunters and most reach the nest by clmbing; so for safety a nest must be either inconspicuous or inaccessible, or if neither it must be protected in some other way.

Inconspicuousness is achieved in a remarkable variety of ways, but hardly ever by the main method used by north-temperate birds. Virtually never in the forest does one find a more or less bulky open nest simply concealed in a thick bush or dense undergrowth. Such a method is evidently far too crude; thick growth of this sort is just what many snakes would find most easy to climb about in. In any case, the sort of thick growth that would be adequate for concealment is rare in undisturbed tropical forest, where the lower growth is usually sparse and not very leafy. Outside the forest, in semiopen bushy country, some birds nest in this way in tropical America as they do in Europe. In the forest not only is the danger from predators very great but the bird also has generally sparser cover in which to conceal its nest. The vegetation is, however, structurally very diverse and a great variety of nest materials is available. The result has been a wealth of very specialized nests, each kind beautifully adapted by its structure and site to elude or deceive the eyes of predators or to foil any attempt to reach it. I can mention only a few of the more outstanding kinds.

A nest can be inconspicuous by being very small. This is the bellbird's solution, and some of the bellbird's relatives have adopted the same strategy. But a tiny platform like the bellbird's nest cannot be built of the first twigs that come to hand; it would never hold together, especially as the bird uses only simple and more or less stereotyped movements when building. So special kinds of twigs must be collected, which will hold together to form a very small but adequately strong structure. As we have seen, the Bearded Bellbird in the Arima Valley used basal twigs of white olivier, and for the central cup the fine forked twigs of the ti-fay. The Calfbird, building the same kind of nest in southern Guyana, used for its base the twigs of *Rinorea brevipes,* and the fine whippy twigs of a species of *Eugenia* for the nest cup. I know of no other cases where the materials used in this kind of nest have been identified; indeed, few such nests have been found. William Beebe found and described the first and only known nest of the Pompadour Cotinga in Guyana in 1924.[31] It was a tiny shallow cup, quite hidden among the breast feathers of the female when she was incubating, so that she appeared to be crouching in the high fork of the bamboo where the nest was placed. The nest itself "consisted solely of a very open, loose tangle of six or eight bits of slender, curly, woody tendrils, forming a deep cup just large enough to hold the egg."

The Rufous Piha, a Central American cotinga, is another extreme example of reduction of the nest to a minimum in the interests of inconspicuousness. Alexander Skutch relates how he found the first of the few nests of this species that have been found.[32] "One day, while walking along a woodland path, I noticed a female piha resting on a slender branch about 20 feet up in a small tree, in an attitude that excited my curiosity. When, after sitting motionless for a long while, the bird flew off, she left exposed a nest so diminutive that it had been largely hidden beneath her. It was a nearly flat pad about three inches in diameter, composed almost wholly of coiled tendrils, and supported by two horizontal twigs no thicker than a lead pencil. Looking up through the meshes of this incredibly light structure, I could see that it held—most precariously, it seemed—a single egg that was smoky gray, heavily mottled with dark brown."

All the birds that are known to build these relatively tiny nests are of thrush size or over. The very inconspicuous nests built by smaller birds are generally very small cups, tiny in themselves but of more normal size for the size of the bird. The manakins and many small antbirds construct fine hammocklike nests, slung in a fork between two diverging horizontal twigs of some low plant. The rim of the nest is secured by strands bound round the supporting twigs and the cup, which hangs in the fork, may be so thin that seen from below the light shines through it. Camouflage is sometimes provided by fragments of dead leaf or moss loosely attached and left hanging below the nest. Many hummingbirds build very small cup nests, but they are felted structures that sit on the top of a twig or small branch. They are secured to the support by cobweb, and they often have pieces of lichen attached to the outside for camouflage.

Other nests are quite bulky, but achieve inconspicuousness through camouflage appropriate to their position. The Pipromorpha,[33] a small forest flycatcher, attaches a bulky covered nest of moss to a hanging rootlet in some shady place beside a bank or a large tree trunk. The nest, about a foot from top to bottom and six inches wide, is in itself not difficult to see, but even if it is quite exposed one may easily pass it by in the shady, mossy place where it hangs. A related bird, the Slaty-capped Flycatcher, suspends its covered nest from a rootlet close under the overhang of a bank or earthfall. It is built of a variety of brown fibrous or cottony plant material, and so blends well with the earth roof above it.

These low hanging nests are not very inaccessible, and camouflage must be important for their protection. Other birds build hanging nests high above the ground, making no attempt to conceal them. Their safety depends simply on in-accessibility. Along the forest paths in Trinidad one often sees dark retort-shaped nests hanging suspended from the tip of a drooping branch in a clear space fifteen or twenty feet above the ground. They are the nests of small flycatchers of the genus *Tolmomyias*, the flatbills. It is difficult to see how even the slenderest snake could climb down to these nests and reach the contents via the downward-pointing spout—yet even so many flatbill nests certainly fail. The hangnests, much larger birds of the family Icteridae, build even more inacces-sible nests, deep pouches with a narrow slit entrance at the side, which they suspend from the outermost twigs of tall trees. Since there is no advantage from concealment, some of the hangnests breed in colonies. The giant trees, festooned with long stocking-shaped nests, with the birds noisily coming and going, are among the most conspicuous objects in the forest.

There is extra safety for any nest, conspicuous or incon-spicuous, that is built in an isolated tree whose crown and trunk stand clear of its neighbors. Monkeys, which must dev-astate many nests as they swing and crash in troupes through the treetops, destroying those that they find and doubtless damaging and dislodging others that they do not find, are much less likely to work through an isolated tree than one that is in contact with its neighbors. Snakes too are probably less likely to visit isolated trees. This is probably the reason why the Bearded Bellbird in Trinidad nests in trees outside the forest edge, and why we found that isolated trees in clearings tended to be good places to look for other nests too. While Barbara was studying the Calfbirds in Guyana I spent a good deal of time watching the Purple-throated Fruit-crow, another large cotinga. The two nests that we found were both within the forest but both in trees that stood clear of their neighbors throughout their length, from the base of the trunk to the crown. Once, when I was watching one of these nests, a troupe of capuchin monkeys passed very close by; and once during the few hours that I was watching the other nest, a troupe of squirrel monkeys passed through the trees nearest to it; but in neither case did they visit the nest tree, to do which they would have had to descend to the ground and then climb the smooth vertical trunk. The first nest was successful, while the second failed, for an unknown reason, after a few days; but neither would have survived a visit from the monkeys.

A few birds of the ovenbird family build such impregnable nests that they have no need to make them inconspicuous. The Ovenbird itself, which builds an enclosed nest of hard mud and places it in an obvious place such as the top of a fence post, lives in open country well to the south of the tropical forest. In the forest, some of its relatives build elaborate fortified nests of masses of sticks, whose central chamber is protected by thick walls and can be entered only by way of a narrow stick tunnel. The contents of such a nest are difficult for even such a large "predator" as man to get at. Instinctively knowing that the safety of the nest depends on its integrity, these birds are constantly at work on their nests, adding new material, and they may even work frantically to repair it while one tries to pick open a small hole in the side in order to see the contents.

Some birds that nest conspicuously gain protection in unorthodox ways. A few species regularly build their nests very close to nests of stinging bees or wasps. The insects appear to get used to the coming and going of the nesting birds and do not molest them, but any creature climbing to the nest and shaking the branches will be immediately attacked. A few species nest conspicuously, but vigorously defend their nests themselves. The most striking instance of this that I have come across myself is the Purple-throated Fruit-crow, mentioned above. I spent many hours watching one of the two nests. The birds made no attempt to avoid drawing attention to the nest, which was placed in the top of a sparsely foliaged tree; but they were so aggressive to any intruders, even hawks, within twenty yards or so of the nest that it was probably safer than if it had been inconspicuous but undefended. They were constantly mobbing any medium-sized or large bird that came near, and as time went by it became obvious that most of the larger birds were keeping clear of the area. Toucans, in particular, kept their distance. The whole social organization of the fruit-crows, in fact, is adapted to such a method of nest protection; they live in small groups of about four to seven birds, and all individuals take part in the care and defense of a single nest. Even the color of their plumage may be connected with this aspect of their behavior. They are entirely black, except that males have a patch of glossy wine red feathers on the throat. Black is a conspicuous color, and in birds tends to be associated with aggressiveness, presumably acting as a warning signal. It is probably no coincidence that the drongos, birds of the Old World tropics, vigorously defend their nests and are also all black.

Hole-nesting forms a subject in itself, and I shall not do more than refer briefly to some of the problems with which the hole-nester has to contend. Generally speaking, holes have the advantage of being fairly safe from predators, but they are difficult to excavate and suitable holes may be much in demand, so that the main danger may be from potential usurpers rather than from predators. But there is great variety in holes, and it is mainly the safe and inaccessible tree holes that are much coveted. Nests in holes in the ground may be rather vulnerable, especially those that are dug in flat or gently sloping ground. Some birds that nest in such holes camouflage their entrance. Nests in holes in rotten stumps and other low places may also be vulnerable. The owners of all such nests tend to behave as secretively when entering or leaving the nest as birds that build in vulnerable open sites.

Hole nests cannot be defended single-handed against would-be usurpers. The parent must leave its nest at times to feed if for no other reason. Consequently the birds that nest in holes all have close pair bonds, and both sexes attend the nest, except for some that live in larger groups and nest communally. Thus the kind of nest that a bird builds may influence its social system. I shall return to this aspect of nesting later, when I try to trace the various threads in the complex web of adaptations by which species survive. I shall end this very sketchy account of nests by considering a rather neglected aspect but one that may be of great importance—the choice of nest material.

The Bearded Bellbird and the Calfbird, as we have seen, choose very specific materials that are especially well suited for interlocking to form their insubstantial and inconspicuous nests. How many trees in the areas where they live could provide twigs with the necessary qualities, for the basal platform and the tenacious nest cup? Could the bellbird, in fact, nest successfully in the Arima Valley of Trinidad if the white olivier and the ti-fay did not grow there? We have no idea. It seemed significant that the Calfbirds which Barbara studied in the Kanukus of southern Guyana had their display and nesting area in a part of the valley where the two trees that provided nest material were particularly abundant; but a very painstaking survey would have been necessary to show whether or not their wider distribution is linked with that of these trees. One can only suggest the possibility—perhaps even the likelihood—that some tropical forest birds may have their distribution determined, at least at the local level, by the distribution of suitable nest materials.

It may be, too, that the availability of nest materials sometimes influences the timing of breeding. In the Arima Valley of Trinidad the Black-and-white Manakin almost always uses for its nest lining the fine branching panicles of a herbaceous forest-edge plant, *Nepsera aquatica* (page 119). This very suitable material forms a tenacious interlocking cup, and it probably has the further advantage that it dries out quickly so that the nest cup does not become sodden after heavy downpours of rain.[34] *Nepsera* seed-heads were available mainly from March to August, but the manakins sometimes began to nest in small numbers up to two months earlier.

The very early nests tended to be lined with other less suitable materials, sometimes finely branched dead grass-heads, which formed a looser nest cup. But I had too few observations to show whether or not these less suitable nest linings influenced the success of the nests. It certainly looked as if the manakins might have tended to delay their nest-building until *Nepsera* was available.

There are some materials on which many species of birds depend. Perhaps the most important is spider's web, which has unique qualities making it an ideal nest-binding material. It is elastic, it adheres to itself and to other things, and it is tough. It is also water-repellent. Many small birds use spider's web liberally to fix the nest to its supporting twigs; the hermit hummingbirds[35] use it to bind the nest to a palm or fern frond, paying out the web and winding it on as they circle round the frond in hovering flight. Hummingbirds and some others use cobweb to bind together the main fabric of the nest, which may consist of moss or other vegetable fragments that do not adhere together by themselves. It is difficult to imagine what would have been the course of hummingbird evolution without spiders.

Many small birds in the tropical forests of the New World build nests very largely of tough black strands that look like coarse horsehair, except that, unlike hair, they are somewhat irregular in width and flattened in cross section rather than cylindrical. They are the hyphae of a fungus, a species of *Marasmius*, that grows on rotten wood.[36] In some areas at least, *Marasmius* seems to be the only readily available material that has the necessary qualities of toughness, flexibility, and durability to enable some species of birds to build their special kinds of nests. The small flycatchers known as flatbills usually build their hanging retort-shaped pouches entirely of *Marasmius*. In Trinidad we once found a nest built of pale grasslike fibers, presumably because the bird had been unable to find a supply of *Marasmius*. It collapsed and fell to the ground before the young had fledged.

If a bird is building a nest of special materials which are not very easy to find, an old nest built of these materials may be a very convenient source of supply and save much time. A nest in active use is equally suitable, if the owner does not defend it adequately. We found, in fact, that some kinds of nests were regularly robbed in this way. It was most striking in the case of Guy's Hermit, a forest hummingbird that Barbara studied.[37] Three species—a flycatcher, another hummingbird, and Guy's Hermit itself—regularly stole, or tried to steal, the material from its nests. Abandoned nests quickly disappeared, while occupied nests needed to be defended constantly from the time that building began. Guy's Hermit builds its nest mainly of soft fibers and "plant down," bound together with cobweb—materials that need patient searching for in their proper places but are particularly easy to pull from a nest in large beakfuls.

Birds' nests are fascinating objects in themselves, and the tropical forest is the best place to study them in their fullest variety. It is a wide open field and one that, like the study of fruit-eating or nectar-eating birds, brings together the ornithologist and the botanist. One can at present only guess at some of the ways in which birds have been influenced in their evolution by the materials which have been available for their nest-building. I shall end with a final speculation, suggesting that in one case at least the influence may not all have been one way.

Obviously birds have had to make do with the materials that happen to be available, materials which have evolved quite independently of their potential use for nest-building. Nobody would suppose that the quality of a spider's web has been evolved so that it should function as a good material for binding nests, nor that the qualities of the twigs of any kind of tree have been influenced by the fact that a bird chooses them for its nest. But the seed-heads of *Nepsera aquatica* may be a special case. All plants have adaptations for dispersal. If the fruiting panicle is undisturbed, *Nepsera* seeds may fall below the plant or at most be blown a little way; it is only if they are taken by a building bird and incorporated in a nest that they are likely to be dispersed any considerable distance. The Black-and-white Manakin in Trinidad is not the only bird that transports them for this purpose. Many other species, birds both of forest and of more open habitats, regularly use them. Yoshika Willis has found that many species of birds in the neighborhood of Belém, at the mouth of the Amazon, use *Nepsera* panicles in their nests; some build almost exclusively of this material.[38] It may be that the fine, springy, branching seed-head of *Nepsera* is adapted for dispersal by birds. If this is so, one wonders whether it is a unique case; or are there other examples of coevolution between birds and the plants that they use for nest material?

9

Oilbirds

Many millions of years ago a nightjarlike bird in South America began to vary its diet in an unusual way. While hawking for flying insects round the forest trees at night it must have taken to occasionally snatching a fruit. The nutritious fruits, rich in protein and fat, on which specialized frugivorous birds depend, must already have been in existence at that time, so that this occasional fruit supplement could have made a useful addition to the nightjar's diet, if taken from the right kind of tree.

From this early beginning arose a unique kind of bird, the Oilbird, a nocturnal fruit-eater which has so many peculiarities that it is placed in a family by itself, but is still recognizably nightjarlike. One of its most remarkable traits is that it spends all day, and nests, deep inside caves, where the absence of light may be so total that a photographic plate may be exposed for hours without being clouded. Most of its peculiarities seem to be a direct consequence of the initial change from a diet of insects to one of fruits; but before speculating further on its evolutionary history it is best to describe the bird itself as it is today.

It is a powerful and impressive bird, about 18 inches long and with a wing span of three to three and a half feet. The beak is strong and hooked, like a hawk's, and surrounded by stiff, forwardly directed bristles, which probably help the bird to locate the eggs and young and any other objects on or near the nest. The tail is long and ample, and folds in an unusual way, in cross-section like an inverted V. The legs are very short and come free of the body very far forward, so that on a flat surface the bird crouches in a down-by-the-head posture, its breast low over its feet and its tail slightly raised. The plumage is rich brown, barred and mottled, with sparse but conspicuous white spots on the wing-coverts and outer wing and tail feathers, and smaller white spots on the head. Males are slightly larger than females and their plumage is a slightly grayer, duller brown, not so richly rufous.

The great naturalist and traveler Alexander von Humboldt discovered the Oilbird for science when he visited Caripe in northern Venezuela in 1799, but it was already well known locally. "That which gives the greatest celebrity to the valley of Caripe," he wrote, "is the great cavern of the Guacharos [Oilbirds]. In a country where people love the marvelous, an inexhaustible subject for conversation is afforded by a cavern that gives birth to a river, and is inhabited by thousands of nocturnal birds the fat of which is used by the missions to prepare food."

Humboldt went on to mention some of the other striking features of the Oilbird: how it leaves the caves only at night to feed on the fruit of forest trees; how its young become very fat; and how the birds make an indescribable clamor when they are disturbed in the caves; "the sharp and piercing sounds are reflected from the rocky vault and the echoes reverberate from the depths of the cavern." Years later it was discovered that one of the calls used in the caves, a clicking noise, serves for echo location. In this respect Oilbirds resemble bats, except that their clicks are easily audible to human ears whereas those of bats are ultrasonic. Several naturalists had suspected that the birds had this ability, but it was not shown experimentally until 1953. Professor D. R. Griffin, the authority on bat sonar, caught a few birds in the Caripe cave, took them to a darkened empty building, and found that they could not avoid obstacles in flight when their ears were plugged. As soon as they were unplugged, however, the same birds could fly about in pitch darkness without hitting anything.[39] It is not yet known how small an object an Oilbird can detect in this way, but certainly their faculty is much cruder than that of bats.

One of the main attractions of the Spring Hill estate in the Arima Valley of Trinidad is that there is a colony of Oilbirds in a cave only ten minutes' walk from the house. It is the most easily accessible colony in Trinidad, and almost certainly in the world, and now that Spring Hill has become internationally known as a nature reserve it has been visited by hundreds of birdwatchers.[40] In 1957, when I went to live in the Arima Valley, it was well known locally, and I began to visit it regularly and to keep detailed notes on the nests, for the Oilbird's breeding habits had never been properly studied.[41]

Most of the Oilbird colonies in Trinidad are in huge caverns. Some are in sea caves which have been hollowed out over the centuries by the surf pounding on the exposed cliffs of the north coast; the others are in limestone caverns in the heights of the Northern Range. In these huge caves the birds nest high up on ledges and in crevices, though this has not prevented poachers from reaching many of the nests by means of ladders cut from the stems of great bamboos, an introduced plant established along many of the streams. The country people in Trinidad have no tradition of boiling down young Oilbirds for their fat, but they consider them good eating. The nests in the sea caves are even less accessible, as the caves can be entered by boat only in the calmest weather. None of them is suitable for regular and detailed study. The Arima Valley cave is the exception. A small stream, one of the upper tributaries of the Arima River, flows down through a steep-sided valley and enters a narrow fissure, through which it descends over a series of small waterfalls until it flows out into the open again about 200 yards further down. In places the cleft is roofed over and becomes a tunnel, and in one of these darker places, not far from the upper entrance, the Oilbirds nest on ledges only 12–15 feet above the stream bed.

I continued my weekly visits to the cave, with few breaks, for four and a half years; at critical periods I sometimes went daily. I shall never forget the kindness and hospitality of Asa Wright, the owner of the estate, and how she welcomed me and regaled me with tea and chocolate cake after I returned from my inspections of the nests. Midafternoon soon became the time for a routine check, not only because of the chocolate cake but because other work was slack by then, once the early afternoon resurgence of display of the manakins was past.

A few simple preparations were necessary before I could get full value from my visits. To descend the first waterfall I needed a short ladder. I made a rough wooden one, but later replaced it with an aluminum ladder, which I kept chained to a tree trunk near the cave mouth as there was always the risk of an occasional poacher. The ladder enabled me not only to descend the waterfall without getting more than my feet wet but also to reach the nests. To study the birds' food I had to collect regular samples of the seeds which they regurgitate while on their nests. Some remain round the edge of the nest, but most fall into the stream below; so I fixed catching trays of wire mesh by driving nails into the sloping rock below some of the nests, emptied them at each visit, and cleared the nests above of any fresh seeds, so that I was able to collect a sample at each visit which I knew was fresh.

I marked the eggs as they were laid, and when there were young birds I ringed them and weighed them regularly, since their growth rate promised to be of especial interest. Finally, in order to be able to watch the birds on their nests from their own level, and not just look up at them from the narrow stream bed, I had a rough wooden platform built between the walls of the gorge a few yards upstream from the nests. This consisted only of two tree trunks jammed into the rock walls, about five feet apart, with planks laid across and surmounted by a small hide. I could reach it by my ladder, and I spent many early morning and late evening hours, and one complete night, sitting on a wooden box on the platform, trying to follow with my less acute senses, and the judicious use of a torch with a red filter, how the better-adapted Oilbirds were spending their time. The platform lasted for nearly four years, but by the end of my time it was becoming rotten and I had to be careful where I put my feet. A year or two later it had vanished, the fragments swept away by the stream which roars in spate through the gorge after every heavy rainfall.

Oilbirds use their nests as a base all the year round, whether they are nesting or not. They rest on them through the day, regurgitating the seeds from the previous night's feed, so that my weekly collections gave a very complete picture of the seasonal succession of trees which the Spring Hill colony exploited. By the end of four and a half years I had sorted and identified well over 100,000 seeds. The birds had generally been said to feed on palm fruits, but in my birds' diet three tree families were of major importance, the palms, the laurel family (Lauraceae), and the incense family (Burseraceae). All these share two main characteristics: the fleshy part of the fruit is rich in fats and proteins—and does not contain much water, so is economical to transport—and there is a single, usually rather large, seed.

Finding the trees to which the seeds in my catching trays belonged was a challenge which kept me intermittently occupied throughout my time in Trinidad. Helpful botanists at Kew and elsewhere made the final identifications of the more difficult species. We took an enthusiastic Dutch botanist, who was on a visit to Trinidad, out into the field for a day and showed him some of our puzzling laurels. He was a specialist in this very difficult family, and he eventually described one of our trees as a new species and identified three others as new records for Trinidad. In the end I knew the names of almost all the trees which the Oilbirds fed at and could find them in the forest. As I also found in studying the fruits which manakins eat, species which are hard to identify from dried specimens in a herbarium may be quite easy as living trees, since their whole appearance, the color of the leaves and the way they are borne, the color and texture of the bark and other characters may all be distinctive, and in addition each may flower and fruit at different times of the year.

Occasionally I was able to watch Oilbirds feeding at one of their food trees at night, circling silently round it with rapid, shallow wing-beats, now and then flying up to the foliage and hovering for a moment to wrench off a fruit. These observations, though few, showed that Oilbirds feed as well as nest socially, for up to five birds would appear at a tree at the same time, and after feeding for a few minutes would all disappear together. Similarly, from my vigils in the cave, I found that several birds would return at about the same time to feed their young, after being absent for two hours or more.

Despite these observations, outside its caves the Oilbird remains relatively unknown. A Venezuelan observer, Dr. Eugenio Pietri, has reported that they occasionally perch on the bare branches of trees, but I never saw this. An occasional bird has been found in the daytime, on the ground or perched in a tree, obviously lost, sometimes a long way from any Oilbird cave. One would like to know much more about how they spend their time when they leave the caves, how they navigate, and how they locate suitable trees with ripe fruit.

They certainly have excellent night vision, and in the open they make no use of the echo-locating clicks which are essential for flight inside the caves. In any case the clicking would probably be of little use in the open with no solid walls to throw back echoes. They range widely over the forest at night in their search for food, and the birds from the different caves probably keep to traditional feeding areas. Thus the birds from two caves five to ten miles east of the Arima Valley regularly took a very large lauraceous fruit, of a tree which grows locally at the eastern end of the Northern Range, but only three seeds of this fruit were found among 112,000 regurgitated in the Spring Hill cave. On the other hand the Spring Hill birds regularly fly at least eight or nine miles to the swampy lowland forest southeast of the Arima Valley, where a certain palm grows on whose fruit they feed a great deal. The Spring Hill birds also regularly take great numbers of fruits of a certain incense tree, which prefers the drier western end of the Northern Range and probably does not extend east of the Arima Valley; its seed was never found among the thousands examined in the caves to the east of the Arima Valley. The Oilbird, from a sea cave on Huevos, one of the islands off the northwest corner of Trinidad, must fly miles for almost all its food, for the forests on the island and within a few miles are of a dry monsoon type, far poorer than those to the east. One of the palms on which the Huevos birds feed probably does not grow within fifteen miles of the cave, and to find another, an introduced species, the birds must visit the gardens and parks of Port-of-Spain, fourteen miles away. Among the many seeds examined in the Huevos cave was a single seed of the very large laurel fruit mentioned above, which almost certainly does not grow within thirty miles of Huevos.

In locating new sources of ripe fruit Oilbirds probably use their sense of smell; but the evidence for this, though strong, is still indirect. In the first place their olfactory organ, and the part of the brain associated with it, is unusually well developed, and it is most unlikely that this would be so unless the sense of smell had an important function. Many of the trees on which Oilbirds feed are, in fact, aromatic, especially those of the laurel and incense families. If one walks beneath such a tree and there is ripe fruit lying on the ground the scent may be very obvious, and it may be equally so to an Oilbird flying past. Once during my study three species of laurels, all with fruits of about the same size, were fruiting abundantly at the same time. Two had fruits that were aromatic to the human nose, one highly so, while the third lacked any aroma. The first two were taken in quantity by the Oilbirds, but among the thousands of regurgitated seeds which I collected over this period there was only a single seed of the third, nonaromatic species.

The palms, one of the main families of food trees, are not aromatic; but while the laurels and incense trees have much the same general appearance as many other forest trees, and their crowns may be crowded in among a lot of others, the palms have a highly distinctive silhouette and their crowns usually stand clear of other trees, so presumably the Oilbirds locate them by sight. With their highly developed night vision, the forest must seem relatively luminous to them on a clear night. Pietri, the Venezuelan observer, mentioned that when he was watching Oilbirds feeding on a moonlit night they alighted on trees when clouds covered the moon, and started feeding again when the moon reappeared. But they can also feed perfectly well on moonless nights.

Outside its caves the Oilbird remains an occasional dark silhouette seen briefly against the night sky, silent except for an occasional harsh call to keep contact with its fellows. Inside the caves it makes a much more powerful impression. In the first place, the noise from a large colony is overwhelming, as Humboldt remarked. The moment the birds are disturbed they begin uttering very loud and harsh snarling and snoring sounds, the more long drawn-out cries reminiscent of the last of the bathwater going down a particularly noisy drain. Some birds begin to leave the ledges and circle round in the half-darkness, faintly lit by the intruding torches. The flashing of a torch beam up to the nest ledges reveals the great birds themselves, some circling round in the vault of the cave with agile flight, others peering suspiciously down from the ledges, their eyes shining red with the reflected torchlight. In places, the floor of the cave is deep with an accumulation of decayed and decaying seeds, supporting a seething mass of cockroaches and other insects and crowned with a small forest of etiolated seedlings which spring up readily in the rich compost but soon wither in the absence of light.

The larger Oilbird caves are among the great ornithological spectacles of the world; but they are not very suitable for finding out in detail about the ecology and behavior of Oilbirds, just as one may learn little by gazing up at a great seabird cliff. I was very lucky to have a small colony, with low and accessible nests, almost at my doorstep. Moreover the Oilbirds at the Spring Hill cave became so used to my visits that the disturbance was slight, which made my visits less dramatic but encouraged me to believe that I was not harming the colony by subjecting it to such close scrutiny. The tamer birds did not leave their nests even when I put the ladder up to within a foot or two of them and climbed up to inspect their eggs or young.

The most striking result of following the nests in the Spring Hill cave week after week was to discover how very prolonged are all the events of the Oilbird's nesting cycle. Most small birds lay the successive eggs of their clutch daily, while larger birds, of about Oilbird size, may lay on alternate days. The interval presumably indicates the length of time needed for each egg to pass through the final stages of development. Oilbirds, on the other hand, lay their eggs at very variable intervals; four or five days is average, six or seven is not uncommon, and I had one record of a nine-day interval between the laying of successive eggs. The laying of a complete clutch, of 2–4 eggs, may therefore take over two weeks. The incubation of each egg takes 33 to 34 days, again a very long time; for the size of the egg a period of around 20 days would be more usual. Since the adults begin to incubate the eggs as they are laid, they hatch at much the same intervals. Finally, the nestling's development is extraordinarily slow for a bird of its size, and again it is very variable. The average age at which I recorded the young birds leaving the nest was nearly 110 days, the extremes being 88 and 125 days. Only some of the larger birds of prey and seabirds have nestling periods as long as this.

Throughout the first 70 days of its long period in the nest the young Oilbird puts on weight, until it is half as heavy again as the adult, about 600 grams to the adult's 400. It becomes extremely fat, and it is at this stage that the missionaries used to collect them at the Caripe cave and boil them down for their oil. Then for the last 30 days or so they lose weight, while their downy covering is replaced by feathers of adult type. There is no juvenile plumage, as there is in almost all other birds. Evidently, since they live in darkness, a distinct juvenile plumage would have no function.

From my hide on the platform spanning the stream I had all the nests in view only a few yards from me. Since the Spring Hill colony is in a gorge which is only partly roofed over, a good deal of daylight reaches the nests and I could see most of what happened by day. At night, however, I had to try to tell what was going on by listening, and by occasional spot-checks with a torch, but this was not very satisfactory as the light disturbed the birds. To get a better idea of what happened at night I attempted to watch through an infrared device known as a snooperscope, or sniperscope, which I obtained as surplus U.S. Army stock. It was a cumbersome machine, powered by a car battery, and so was a good deal of trouble to carry up and down the steep and slippery slopes to the cave. If I had been able to get really clear views through it of the Oilbirds at their nests it would have been well worth it, but in fact the image was poor and the field of view very narrow; I could just about see the birds but could not see in detail what they were doing. I abandoned it after a few trials; but years afterward Jan Lindblad, the Swedish wildlife photographer, used a much more advanced instrument with which he obtained excellent photographs of the Spring Hill Oilbirds feeding their young in pitch darkness.

My simpler methods were not wholly ineffective, however. Careful listening, combined with occasional judicious use of the torch with a red filter, which reduced the disturbance, enabled me to get a good idea of what went on at night at the nests. For most of the day the birds are inactive, perched in pairs on their nests; for much of the time they sleep or doze. Toward evening, which comes early in the tropics, there is an increase in activity and birds begin to leave their nests and fly around, calling and clicking. This period of restlessness lasts for an hour or more before the departure from the cave begins. At about 6 P.M. they begin to leave, and half an hour or so later all the adults have gone, except that if there are any with small young in the nest one of the parents remains behind.

The small number of Oilbirds in the Spring Hill cave could leave by three ways, up the gorge, down the gorge, or by a top entrance, and so their departure was not easy to record exactly. But the two hundred or so birds in the Oropouche cave, a large limestone cave about ten miles east of Spring Hill, have to leave through a single small entrance, after negotiating a long narrow passage. We watched one evening at the mouth of this cave and counted the birds as they emerged. The departure lasted over an hour and a half. It was obvious that some birds were showing hesitation before coming out into the open, and that the entrance passage was acting as a bottleneck. We could hear them, one or two at a time, clicking as they flew down the passage toward the cave mouth, and then turned and flew back up the passage. As soon as they finally emerged into the open the clicking stopped and they disappeared into the night.

At the Spring Hill cave the first birds with young in the nest began to return to feed them at about 9 P.M. In the course of one complete night that I spent on the platform over the gorge, I recorded three main feeding periods, starting at 1:30, 3:40 and 5:30 A.M., during which it seemed that every nestful of young was fed, and there were three minor feeding periods when only one or two nests were visited. The adults arrived so much at the same time that it seemed certain that they must have been foraging in company. It was not difficult to record the return of an adult, in spite of the total darkness. The bird could be heard clicking as it entered the cave and flew round. The clicks would accelerate as it approached the cave wall and slow down as it turned away into a more open part of the cave. Finally, the clicks would accelerate sharply and then suddenly stop as the bird flew up to its nest and landed.

As it grew light, at about 6 A.M., the last feeding was still in progress, and I could just see the birds at the better-illuminated nests. When begging for food, the young squeal shrilly and crane their heads up toward the parent. When they are being fed, they half-turn their heads so that their beaks interlock with the parent's beak. The shrill begging calls cease abruptly at the moment the beaks interlock. As the adult regurgitates food, its head and that of the nestling with it move in short quick jerks. At nests with large young the process of feeding is most vigorous; in the half-light these nests appear to be filled with a heaving mass of birds: adult and young push strenuously during the feeding, with beaks interlocked, and may rear up together with the chick's head pointing obliquely upward and the adult's downward. The adults seem to be under great physical strain and push with

Circling silently around a food tree at night

their feet and sometimes flap their wings to avoid falling backward. In this attitude parent and chick may rear and heave together for a minute or more.

Because each stage of the nesting cycle is so slow a complete nesting, from the laying of the first egg to the flying of the last young, lasts for five months or more. The pairs do not all begin to nest at the same time, and if a nest fails the female may lay again, with the result that there is hardly any time of the year when some nesting is not in progress at an Oilbird colony. Nevertheless the Spring Hill colony had a definite season: the main period of egg-laying began in December and continued until May; few new clutches were started from June to September, and I recorded no egg-laying in October and November. Some pairs which started early succeeded in raising a second family in the same year. Nearly half of all the nesting attempts were successful, so that a constant succession of young birds was produced.

Altogether, sixty young birds were raised in the four years of my study, by a breeding population which varied from eight to thirteen pairs. And yet not one of these young birds, all of which I ringed, remained in the cave for long after they had left the nest. I did not systematically ring the adults, as I found that catching unsettled them for some time afterward and I did not want them to be made shy. But one adult which I ringed in 1958 remained in occupation of the same nest for at least twelve years afterward. It seems that for Oilbirds, as for other tropical forest birds, life is rather safe for the adult, but young birds probably suffer a very heavy mortality.

In a small cave like the Spring Hill gorge the number of Oilbirds which can take up residence, and certainly the number of pairs that can breed, must depend very strictly on the number of suitable ledges. When these are all occupied there is no room for young birds to settle, until an old bird dies. In addition to the difficulty which a young bird must usually have in, literally, securing a niche for itself in a cave, its first ventures out of the cave at night must be hazardous. It is not known whether young birds are fed at all by their parents once they have left the nest.

This chapter began with a few rather speculative statements about the evolution of the Oilbird. Though it is most unlikely that a series of fossils will ever be found which will enable us to trace its ancestry with certainty, the most likely course of its evolution can be reconstructed by indirect means, and I make no apology for doing this, speculative though such an exercise is, for the evolution of the Oilbird is very relevant to one of the main themes of this book, the consequences of eating fruit.

The second half of the nineteenth century saw a great proliferation of anatomical studies of birds, stimulated by Darwin's *Origin of Species*. The aim was to trace the evolutionary relationships of the various orders and families of birds, and the method was to describe and compare as many of the organ systems of birds as possible—skeleton, musculature, digestive organs, vocal organs, to name but a few. As soon as specimens became available of the Oilbird they were eagerly examined, and the outcome of the examination was that Oilbirds appeared to be most closely related to the nightjars and allied birds but also showed some affinity, though less close, to the owls. No further progress was made until 1960, when Dr. Charles Sibley of Yale University began to analyze the egg-white proteins of birds in an ambitious effort to provide an independent, and perhaps more fundamental, basis for classifying birds by arranging them according to the similarity of their constituent proteins. I sent him a sample of the egg white of an Oilbird and his analysis showed, in agreement with the anatomical evidence, that Oilbirds are closest to the nightjars but also show some similarities to the owls.[42]

Both lines of evidence, from anatomy and from the submicroscopic level of proteins, thus indicate that the Oilbird's ancestry lies within the stock that gave rise to the present-day nightjars, or perhaps among the ancestors of the owls. A consideration of feeding behavior strongly suggests that the ancestor was in fact a nightjarlike bird rather than owllike. Both nightjars and Oilbirds feed on the wing, seizing their food—insects and fruit, respectively—in the beak and swallowing it whole. The owls, on the other hand, seize their prey with their talons and tear it to pieces with the beak. The transition from the nightjar's method of feeding to the Oilbird's is an easy one, just a question of what food is taken; but from an owl's to an Oilbird's feeding method would be a most unlikely evolutionary change.

That there was a variety of nutritious fruits available when the ancestral Oilbird began to change its diet seems clear. Oilbirds are found only in the Andes, from Peru northward, along the eastern extension of the Andes in Venezuela (of which Trinidad is an outlier), and in the Guiana highlands, and there is no evidence that their distribution has ever been wider. Fruits of the sort that they feed on are found, however, all over the New World tropics and are eaten by many other kinds of birds. These nutritious fruits have almost certainly evolved in close relation to the birds which disperse their seeds, as I have argued in an earlier chapter; but their origin is clearly more ancient than the Oilbird's. In any case the Oilbird is not an efficient disperser of their seeds, as it regurgitates most of them within dark caves. Why one sort of nightjar, out of many, took this evolutionary road we shall never know; but once it had begun to eat fruit in significant quantities certain consequences must have followed, profoundly altering its social behavior and its nesting.

Nightjars, like most other insectivorous birds, are territorial and live in pairs during the breeding season. The main defense of their nests against predators lies in their inconspicuousness, and in the fact that they are well dispersed. In fact they build no nest in the usual sense but lay their eggs on the bare ground, against which the sitting adult and the chick are beautifully camouflaged. Like other insectivorous birds they forage individually, not in flocks, since there is no advantage in banding together when hunting for flying insects, a source of food which is usually fairly evenly dispersed.

Fruit-eating birds, on the other hand, tend to feed socially, since fruit tends to be patchy in its distribution but, once found, is usually abundant. This is especially the case in the tropical forest where there may be hundreds of different kinds of trees only a few of which, at any particular time, may have ripe fruit of a suitable kind. When one source of fruit is exhausted it may be difficult to find a new source, and it is a great advantage for an individual bird not to be dependent solely on its own efforts in locating each new source of fruit as it becomes available. This difference in foraging strategy between insectivorous and frugivorous birds is a very fundamental one, exemplified in many different families, and it seems certain that as the ancestral Oilbird began to switch to a diet of fruit there must have been strong pressure on it toward a more thoroughgoing social behavior. If it was originally territorial, as is probable, its territorial tendencies must have begun to decline.

At the same time it must have encountered increasing difficulties over its nesting. Almost certainly its ancestor was a ground-nester and laid its eggs in the open, relying on camouflage. But birds which eat fruit themselves and feed their young on fruit, the seeds of which are regurgitated, cannot nest inconspicuously on the ground, for piles of seeds are bound to accumulate round the nest site. The fruit-eating cotingas do not come up against this difficulty as they nest in trees and the seeds that fall to the ground below do not give away the nest. I had the impression, however, that some of my manakin nests that were only a foot or two above the ground might have been endangered by the piles of seeds below the nest, which might well have attracted a predator's attention. Other fruit-eating birds, such as toucans, nest in tree holes, where the regurgitated debris does not matter. The evolving Oilbird must have been forced to change its nest site, and it seems most likely that it took to nesting on cliff ledges, where it gained its main protection from inaccessibility and not from camouflage. No other course, in fact, seems possible as a first step in the direction which it was to follow.

The need to nest on cliff ledges must have restricted the ancestral Oilbird's range to mountainous country, whatever it may have been before, and it must also have encouraged it to begin to nest socially, as cliffs are few and far between and one pair nesting on a cliff is not endangered by others nesting nearby. In all families of birds cliff-nesters are social nesters, except for some birds of prey which need large individual feeding territories. It is interesting that there is one other fruit-eating bird which has diverged in its nesting habits from the rest of its family and illustrates one of the stages that must have been passed through by the evolving Oilbird. The Cock-of-the-rock, as we have seen, nests on rock faces and there may be several nests within a few yards of each other. To pick another striking example, the Andean Hill-star, the hummingbird that nests higher than any other in the Andes, attaches its nest to irregularities of the rock face in small sheltered caves, and again—most unusually for a hummingbird—several may nest within a few yards of one another.

It was probably at this stage that the ancestral Oilbird began to develop the faculty of echolocation, since this would have been of obvious value in flying round and landing on cliffs at night. Probably, too, it began to make use of regurgitated seed matter and perhaps semidigested fruit pulp to build up a flatter platform on which to nest and so make the cliff ledges safer for the eggs and young. But nest sites must always have been at a premium, and there must have been an immense advantage in being able to penetrate deeper into caves and crevices in the cliffs. The increasing efficiency of echolocation must eventually have allowed the birds to do this, until they were able to penetrate into the vast interior chambers of great cave systems and so were able to take advantage of a wealth of new nest sites which were completely safe, until the arrival of man.

Nightjars and other nightjarlike birds lay only one or two eggs. Almost certainly the Oilbird's large family size, of up to four, is closely linked with the very slow rate of development of the young. For most birds, whose young are subjected to predation, it seems that the length of time the young are in the nest has been reduced to a minimum, and since rapid development means rapid feeding this may set an upper limit to the number of young that can be reared. When the ancestral Oilbird took to nest sites that were safe from predators, this restraint was lifted and it became possible to rear a larger family more slowly. Slow development may also be necessitated by the diet. Although the fruits on which Oilbirds feed are, for fruits, very rich in proteins, it is not known whether they provide the right kinds of amino acids—the constituents from which proteins are built up—in sufficient quantity to allow a more rapid development. The fact that the intervals between the laying of successive eggs are so long suggests that the diet may not allow a more rapid development of eggs, and so there may be a limit too to the rate at which the young can grow.

The high fat content of the fruit is obviously responsible for the great quantity of fat which the young Oilbirds lay down. Fat provides energy but is not of direct use, as protein is, in building up new tissues. There is, however, a limit to the rate at which energy can be used up, and in the early stages of the nestling period, when the young Oilbird is rather inactive, much more fat is provided in the diet than can be burnt up, and it accumulates. It may be useful at this stage, in conjunction with the nestling's thick coat of down, in providing insulation in the comparatively cool conditions of the caves. Later, as the young become more active and the feathers begin to grow, the fat is used up, until the young bird fledges at about the same weight as the adult. It may be that the speed with which the accumulated fat can be used up is another factor affecting the length of time that the young remain in the nest.

All these factors—diet, safety of the nest, family size, rate of development, and the fat deposits—are causally interrelated, but it is not easy to disentangle the relationships. It does violence to the complexity of the adaptive web to "explain" one factor by reference to some other single factor. One can be fairly certain, nevertheless, that the original change in diet from insects to fruit was the historical starting point which led to the Oilbird's unique breeding adaptations as we see them today.

10

The Web of Adaptation

Feeding habits, social behavior, nesting, anatomy, plumage—in any bird all are interconnected, each affects the others in various ways. Some of the connections can be traced, doubtless there are others which we cannot yet guess at. One cannot fully understand any aspect of a bird's natural history in isolation; but the web is so complicated that it is difficult to know how to tackle it—which thread to follow first. Some of the connections have been traced in previous chapters; here an attempt is made to see the web as a whole. It will involve some repetition, but this is necessary to the development of the argument.

A species living in a tropical forest is faced with a multitude of "choices": what it should eat, how it should nest, where it should roost, and so on. In order to survive, it must choose wisely; there are so many competitors and predators that any mistake will be severely penalized. Needless to say, the bird does not really choose; the course that it takes is determined by its past evolutionary history, the opportunities offered by the environment, and the competitors and predators with which it has to contend. Natural selection guides it. But it is a convenient mental shorthand to use the word "choice," and to think of the totality of choices made by a bird as its "strategy" for survival.

The most basic choice of all is what to eat. Let us consider only the two main kinds of food eaten by the cotingas and manakins, and by the majority of all other forest birds: insects and fruit. Insects are generally difficult to find, or at least a good deal of time must be spent in catching them. They tend to be fairly evenly distributed through the environment. Consequently, if insects are a bird's main choice it will probably be an advantage to be able to forage over a largish area without much competition from others of the same species, it is unlikely that a great deal of time can be devoted to other activities such as display, and it is likely to be necessary for both male and female to feed the young. An effective strategy for such a bird will be to live in pairs and maintain a territory. If, on the other hand, fruit forms the main part of the diet, the consequences are likely to be very different. Fruit is easy to obtain when available, but in the forest it is patchily distributed. For a fruit-eating bird there is thus a great advantage in social feeding, and correspondingly little advantage in holding a territory. Fruit, once located, may be obtained in a short time, so that much of its day may be spent in other activities; and the female may be able to find enough food to rear her young unaided, especially if a small family size is advantageous for other reasons. One of the consequences of all this—and a main theme of this book—is that some groups of fruit-eating birds have evolved a specialized social system; the males spend most of their time in courtship display, while the females undertake all the nesting duties.

Moreover, a diet of fruit not only provides the conditions which favor the evolution of conspicuous adornments in males, it also directly enables them to produce bright plumage. Birds cannot synthesize red and yellow pigments, but assimilate them from their food and lay them down essentially unaltered in their feathers. For forest birds, fruits are the main source of these pigments.[43]

Of course it is a gross oversimplification to present the

choice of possible diets simply as one between insects and fruit, but it is helpful to start by considering the extremes. Many birds eat both insects and fruit, and much depends on what kinds are eaten, and—in the case of insects—how they are obtained. Moreover insectivorous birds have some special ways of exploiting their food supply in addition to foraging alone or in pairs. They frequently feed in mixed parties, of many species together, which move through the forest, each bird searching the vegetation in its own manner but apparently getting an advantage from the general disturbance and movement of insects caused by all the others, and perhaps also from the more efficient warning of approaching predators provided by many pairs of eyes. A few species, the ant-followers, rely almost entirely on army ants for their food, accompanying the ant swarms closely and seizing the insects and other small creatures that the ants flush from the cover of the forest floor. But the ant-followers are basically territorial birds and do not accompany the ant columns far beyond the boundaries of their territory, and the same is probably true of most of the birds that forage in mixed flocks.

Food is all-important, but it is not the only factor that shapes a bird's strategy for survival. The choice of nest and nest site also has far-reaching consequences. Again we must oversimplify, and broadly divide nests into a few main adaptive types; more details are given in chapter 8. For most small and medium-sized forest birds the most important requirement of the nest is that it should be as safe as possible from predators. To achieve this end, it may be either inconspicuous or inaccessible (some nests manage to combine both qualities). Inconspicuous nests tend to be either very small and flimsy, such as those of some cotingas, or camouflaged in some way, in which case they may be quite bulky. It is also important that birds attending the nest should themselves be inconspicuous, both in appearance and behavior. Inaccessible nests tend to be either built in an inaccessible position, for instance attached to the end of a hanging branch, or placed in some sort of hole, or fortified in some way, for example by being made of thorny twigs or hard mud. In the latter case the result is not unlike hole-nesting, the bird making its own hole. For birds that nest in such ways it is much less important, or even not important at all, that the parents attending the nest should be inconspicuous.

There is a further complication. The kind of nest that a bird can build may be determined to some extent by its feeding habits. The hangnests, a large New World family with many forest species, have sharply pointed beaks; they feed by probing and piercing, taking nectar and insects from flowers and juice from fruits. It is undoubtedly their finely pointed beaks that enable them to construct the beautifully woven pouches of fine strands for which the family is so notable, and thereby to rely for the safety of their nests on slinging them from the outer twigs of high trees. At the other extreme, the wide froglike gape of a bellbird is ill-adapted to fine work and its twig nest is made by simple side-to-side movements, whereby the bird manages to work suitable twigs, with the right degree of flexibility and sufficient notches for interlocking, into a small and thin but adequately strong platform. The nightjars, also with wide mouths and short beaks—but for catching insects, not for swallowing whole fruits—build no nest; so that when the ancestral Oilbird had to move to a safer nest site than the open ground its only course was to take to cliff ledges. This part of the web of adaptations was laid down in the distant past, when the different families of birds were evolving their general characters.

The choice of nest type, in conjunction with diet, has all sorts of consequences for a bird. Consider first insect-eating birds which nest inconspicuously. Such birds are typically territorial, both sexes attend the nest, and the male is not very brightly colored. The bird's appearance, its general behavior, and its social responses are all conditioned by the two overriding requirements of diet and nest. For insect-eating birds that nest inaccessibly, some of the conditions are similar but there are important differences. In the first place their nest sites, if natural (such as tree holes), are likely to be much in demand, and not only by members of their own species. Secondly, since the safety of the nest does not depend on its being inconspicuous the birds need not be inconspicuous either. As a consequence, such birds tend to have very close pair bonds (because one bird alone cannot defend the nest site against potential usurpers), male and female are not very different in appearance (because their roles are similar), and both may be brightly colored. And incidentally, if they are strictly insectivorous the bright colors are likely to be mainly structural and not pigmentary—white, iridescent purples, blues, and greens, not red, orange, and yellow.

For fruit-eating birds, the choice of nest site has the same general consequences as it does for insectivorous birds, but diet also plays a part. If the young are fed entirely or mainly on fruit, large amounts of it must be brought to the nest, and masses of seeds are regurgitated. If the nest is in a hole the accumulation of seeds does not matter, but it could be a danger to any nest depending on inconspicuousness for its safety, especially to any nest on or near the ground. I often wondered whether some of the very low nests of Black-and-white Manakins were endangered by the little piles of seeds and fruit debris on the ground only two or three feet beneath them. It is probably for this reason, as I have argued, that the ancestral Oilbird was forced to change from ground-nesting to nesting on inaccessible ledges. Most of the fruit-eating cotingas solve the problem by nesting inconspicuously at a considerable height, so that the seeds that fall and are scattered on the ground below offer little clue to the nest's whereabouts.

The connection between diet, social organization, and nest type is well illustrated by the cotingas. Most of the large, more or less frugivorous species with conspicuous males nest inconspicuously, the female being cryptically colored. One, the Cock-of-the-rock, has a bulky and conspicuous nest, but it is inaccessible. In these species the males take no part in nesting. There are however three species that nest in holes in trees, the tityras. In marked contrast to the others, they live strictly in pairs, apparently throughout the year; and the females are not much less conspicuous than the males. There is ample evidence showing that the tityras need to be constantly vigilant in defending their nest holes from potential usurpers. One other group of species nests very differently from the others. The becards are small, largely insectivorous cotingas. They build bulky and conspicuous covered nests, which depend for safety mainly on being inaccessible. Thus they are attached to terminal twigs of large trees or placed in high forks, or—in at least one species—are built near to nests of stinging bees. Like the tityras, both sexes attend the nest, but the pair bond is not so close and permanent as in the tityras, presumably because cooperation between the sexes is needed in feeding the young but not for constantly defending the nest against usurpers.

Another set of strands in the web of adaptations connects feeding habits and nest type with family size. Here some of the interpretations are more controversial, though the main facts are clear enough. I shall not be able to do more than give a brief and necessarily oversimplified sketch of the salient facts and possible interpretations.

One of the striking facts about the nesting of tropical birds is that they lay small clutches of eggs compared with birds of higher latitudes. This has been known for a long time, and a common interpretation has been that tropical species are not able to feed so many young as their counterparts at higher latitudes because the tropical day is shorter than spring and summer days in the north and so less time is available for foraging. But it seems unlikely that the difference in daylength alone can account for the full extent of the change in family size with latitude, and a supplementary explanation has been put forward: that in the tropics the availability of food for birds shows less seasonal fluctuation than at high latitudes. This is certainly true in humid parts of the tropics, where there is nothing to correspond with the great flush of insect and other food during the breeding season of northern birds. In support of this explanation it has been found that in the tropics clutch sizes are on average a little higher in open habitats, where there is probably a greater seasonal change in insect and other bird foods between the dry and wet seasons, than in adjoining forest where seasonal changes are less marked.

The amount of food which parent birds can supply to their young is obviously of crucial importance in setting an upper limit to family size. Many studies of northern birds have shown that family size is very finely adjusted to it; indeed a large part of the literature on bird ecology has been devoted to working out the details of this adjustment. The availability of food must set an upper limit to the number of young that tropical birds too can rear; but I believe that in the tropical forest, at least, family size is as a rule kept below that limit by other factors.

When the significance of clutch size in birds was first being widely discussed about twenty-five years ago, Alexander Skutch, by far the most experienced ornithologist in tropical America, pointed out that species in which both male and female feed the young do not, on average, have larger families than related species in which only the female feeds the young.[44] He drew his examples from the large family of tyrant-flycatchers. He also gave examples showing that if for some reason a bird has been prevented from feeding its young for some time it can compensate, apparently very easily, by increasing its rate of bringing food to the nest very greatly above the normal rate. These facts, especially the first, seem to me to throw much doubt on the adequacy of the usual explanation of low clutch sizes in the tropics. A single instance of course proves nothing; but my doubt was strongly reinforced when I was studying the Purple-throated Fruit-crow in Guyana and watched four adults all feeding the single nestling, sometimes as many as three of them "queueing up" to deliver their food and regularly offering it more than it could eat.[45] It was impossible to believe that two or more young could not have been adequately fed. It was nearly as hard to believe that the Bearded Bellbird in Trinidad, which fed its single nestling only eleven times in the course of a whole day, and evidently spent only a small part of each day in foraging, could not have provided enough food for two young.

It is indeed difficult to make sense of the family size of tropical forest birds if one leaves out of account a most important factor: the nest. We first became convinced of this during our field work in Trinidad, for the species with which we became familiar provided plenty of clues. Many species in the large tyrant-flycatcher family build open cup-nests, and nearly always lay a clutch of two eggs. Other species build larger closed nests of various kinds, and they commonly lay clutches of three eggs. Of the tanagers, nearly all the species build open nests and lay two eggs, but one common species builds a covered nest which it places in a niche, rather like a Wren's nest, and it lays four or sometimes even five eggs. As a broad generalization, one can say that most of the forest birds of the American tropics that build open nests lay clutches of two eggs, and some of the larger species only a single egg; larger clutches are laid mainly by species that build closed nests, or nests in holes or in other kinds of protected sites. The relation between size of clutch and nest type is most striking when comparisons are made between fairly closely related birds.

Open nests in tropical forests are in constant danger; only a small fraction ever survive to produce fledged young. The bird's best strategy is to make its nest as inconspicuous as possible—which usually means as small as possible, and to make its own visits to and departures from the nest as inconspicuous as possible—which means that it must not approach or leave the nest more often than it needs. Any device which reduces the chance of the nest being discovered by only a little will bring a great advantage, even if the result is that the family size has to be reduced. Imagine a case where only 10 percent of the nests of a certain species are successful (a normal figure in tropical forests). If it can in some way reduce the 90 percent of nests that are destroyed to 80 percent—a reduction of only 10 percent—the number of successful nests will be doubled, from 10 percent to 20 percent. In other words, when nest losses are very high a slight reduction in them will have a disproportionate effect on the number of young successfully reared. This simple fact of arithmetic is, I think, most important for understanding nesting adaptations in the tropical forest; it helps to explain why it may be better to build a very small nest, which can hold only two young, than a larger nest which could hold three or four.

In the hypothetical case mentioned above, a reduction in nest losses from 90 percent to 80 percent would double the nesting success. This enables one to understand how it may be an advantage to make the ultimate reduction in clutch size, from two eggs to one; it may be better to build a minute nest which can hold only one nestling, if such a nest is a little more

likely to survive than a larger one. This is what the Bearded
Bellbird seems to have done.

The upper limit to family size which must be set, for any
species, by the amount of food which the parent or parents
can bring to the nestlings, is probably a good deal lower in
tropical forests than in temperate regions. There is no reason
to suppose that this limit is not reached by some hole-nesting
birds, and by some others whose nests are safe from predation.
Of the cotingas only the tityras, which nest in holes, and the
becards, which build bulky covered nests, are known to lay
more than two eggs. Few tityra clutches have been examined,
as their nests are usually inaccessible, but three seems to be the
usual number of eggs. The becards normally lay three or four
eggs. Four also seems to be the upper limit of clutch size for
the tropical woodpeckers, and, to take a very different bird,
for the Oilbird too. It may be that in the tropical forest the
most usual upper limit to family size set by the availability
of food is four, which is a good deal below the limit set for
birds of higher latitudes.

Food is not the only factor which may set an upper limit,
theoretical or real, to family size. For every kind of nest there
is an upper limit to the number of young that it can safely hold,
set by its physical properties. It is not always easy, or indeed
possible with existing knowledge, to decide in individual cases
which is setting the limit. Oilbirds, whose nests are safe from
almost all natural predators, have an upper limit of four, as
already mentioned. Four full-grown Oilbirds, with one or two
parents, completely fill a nest, and if they were to lay more
eggs they might well produce, on average, no more young because some would fall off, whether adequately fed or not. To
take another example, the hangnests of the New World tropics
build beautifully woven closed pouches, slung inaccessibly
from the outermost branches of large trees. They make no
attempt to make their nests inconspicuous. They do not as a
rule, however, lay more than two eggs, and the most likely
reason is that an adult bird with two well-grown young is as
much as this kind of nest can safely hold. To take one more
example from a very different family: in Trinidad we
examined a large number of nests of two species of swifts.[46]

One, the Short-tailed Swift, nests in holes or caves, nowadays mainly in man-made structures like the Chimney Swift of North America. It lays clutches of four or five eggs, occasionally even six. The nest is a very small bracket, the shape of half a saucer, fixed to a vertical wall or rock face. It could not possibly hold four or five well-grown young birds; but when the nestlings are still quite small and unfeathered they leave the nest and cling to the wall beside or below it, where they remain until they can fly. The Chestnut-collared Swift has a more specialized choice of nest site: it attaches a bracket-shaped structure, made of different materials but with about the same sized nest cup as the Short-tailed Swift's nest, to a vertical rock face beside or overhanging a waterfall or hill stream. It would not be possible for the young to cling to the smooth, often damp and overhanging rock face to which the nest is attached. Accordingly the Chestnut-collared Swift lays only one or two eggs, and the young remain on the nest until they fly. Even for two fully grown young there is barely standing room on the nest.

Once they have passed the dangerous early stages of life, tropical forest birds can expect to live a long time, compared with land birds of temperate and high latitudes. The Black-and-white Manakin provided the first proof of this, and more recent studies are beginning to show the same thing. A moment's reflection shows that it must be so. If a population is to remain stable—and if man does not interfere, most bird populations remain more or less stable over the years—a low reproductive rate must be matched by a low mortality rate. But the chain of cause and effect is not so easy to get at. Do the adults live long because only a few young birds are added to the population each year; in other words, because the pressure from new members of the population, competing with them and displacing them, is low? Or do they produce few young because their lives are long and they need produce only small numbers of young each year in order to balance their losses? Both explanations have been put forward, and they reflect fundamentally opposing views as to the means by which animal populations are regulated. The former explanation is based on the idea that natural selection must always ensure that in any animal population the highest effective reproductive rate is always achieved, and that the mortality rate is ultimately a consequence of the reproductive rate. This is logically a very sound idea, because reproductive rates must surely be more directly subject to natural selection than any other aspect of an animal's life: if some individuals contribute more to future generations than other individuals, surely the genetic attributes of the former must quickly displace the latter's. It is difficult to see how natural selection could ever favor individuals that reproduce more slowly than they might.[47]

The second explanation is based on the idea that reproductive rates are somehow adjusted so as to balance the mortality. This is, for the reasons just given, a difficult position to maintain, because it implies that the reproductive rate must often be held lower than it might be. Proponents of this view have had to argue that, in determining reproductive rates, natural selection operates not on the individual but on the local population: those populations that do not overbreed and thus overexploit their resources are at an advantage over those that do, and will eventually displace them.[48]

I cannot resolve this problem, which has been debated by ecologists for a generation; but I think that the arguments on both sides have tended to overlook the possibility—in birds at any rate—that the general nature of the environment in which they live may promote both a high adult survival and a low reproductive rate, or vice versa, independently of any effect that one of these may have on the other. For instance, tropical forest birds live in an environment that is rather stable throughout the year, and extremely rich in species, both of plants and animals; in an environment, that is to say, where drastic changes in food supply or in the hazards of life are unlikely. It is an environment in which any defenseless organism is in great danger of being eaten by one of the multitudes of creatures that are adapted to exploit every possible source of food, but in which a mobile animal, with a highly developed brain and quick reactions, can live rather safely. Whatever the means may be whereby its population remains in balance over the years, a tropical forest bird would be expected to have a high rate of adult survival and a low reproductive rate. We may contrast this with a north European bird, whose food supply alters drastically with the seasons, unless it migrates—in which case it faces other hazards—but which breeds when food is very abundant and in an environment containing a far smaller variety of predators than the tropical forest. Whatever the means by which its population might be regulated, such a species would be expected to have a low rate of adult survival and a high reproductive rate. We may generalize and say that in any complex and weakly seasonal environment adult survival rates will be high and reproductive rates low, and the opposite will be the case in poorer, highly seasonal environments.

At the risk of making the whole thing seem far too involved —a risk that I take, because the truth is undoubtedly much more complicated than this oversimplified sketch—I must point out another way in which adult survival and reproductive rates may be linked. If a bird has a good chance of living a long time once it has reached maturity, it has much to gain from even slight reductions in the risks to which it exposes itself. And the gain, in years of further life, increases more and more rapidly for each percentage increase in its chance of surviving from one year to the next. Thus if it can increase its chance of annual survival from 60 percent to 70 percent, its expectation of life increases from 2 to 2.8 years; a further increase, from 70 percent to 80 percent, increases the expectation of life from 2.8 to 4.5 years; and another increase, from 80 percent to 90 percent, increases the expectation of life from 4.5 to 9.5 years. I found that adult Black-and-white Manakins in Trinidad have an annual survival rate of about 90 percent, and later studies have produced similar figures for other tropical forest birds; so these calculations are not simply hypothetical.

Now nesting is certainly one of the activities in which a bird puts itself at risk. It imposes a greater physiological strain than usual, it involves the relaxation to some degree of a bird's attention to the dangers of predation and other hazards, and a bird on the nest, especially at night, is probably at greater risk from predation than it would otherwise be. Ringing studies have shown that the adults of some British birds suffer heavier mortality during the breeding season than they do even at the height of winter. Northern birds, however, which anyway have a high annual mortality and a poor expectation of life but can breed prolifically, have little to gain and much to lose by lowering their reproductive potential in the interests of their own safety. But a tropical forest bird has much to gain by doing everything possible to reduce the risks involved in nesting; it stands to gain very little from each attempt to breed, since most of its attempts fail and few young are produced when it does succeed. In such circumstances it is very sound strategy to minimize the risks of breeding and thereby improve the chance of a longer life. There are three ways in which a bird may do this: by attempting to nest only when conditions are most favorable; by not breeding until it is thoroughly experienced; and by not attempting to rear too large a family. Small birds of the tropical forest have, it seems, made use of all these means of improving their expectation of life. Their breeding tends to be irregular in its timing, and such studies as have been made indicate that this is in response to the suitability of local conditions. They do not, on average, begin to breed at such a young age as birds living in temperate regions or in highly seasonal parts of the tropics. Their small family size we have already considered, as one of the means of reducing the risks to which so many nests are exposed. The emphasis then was on the survival of the eggs or young, but it must have an effect on the survival of the parent too. The energy saved by producing only two eggs instead of three or four and feeding correspondingly few young, must allow a bird more time to exercise the skill and vigilance that enable it to survive.

For every bird species the web of adaptations is different; and for no species can we do more than make a very tentative, provisional sketch of the web. Only a few aspects of the natural history of a few species have been so thoroughly studied that one can define with some certainty the part that they play in the bird's strategy for survival. In many cases observation alone, however prolonged, is not enough; field experiments must be carried out as well, to provide the alternative conditions that the bird would not otherwise experience. It was only by moving eggshells about themselves and putting them where they wanted them that Niko Tinbergen and his coworkers could show how important it is for the Black-headed Gull that it should remove the shells from its nest as soon as the young have hatched. In tropical forests such work has not yet started.

Specialists are sometimes accused of finding out more and more about less and less. In some subjects the charge may perhaps be justified, if there is any subject in which the detail is either trivial or of no significance beyond itself. I can think of such subjects, but this may only reflect my ignorance of them. Some ornithologists even, mostly those of the older school concerned mainly with the classification and distribution of birds, criticize others for spending all their time "counting how many times a bird flicks its tail"—it is usually put in this sort of way, to emphasize the triviality of the exercise. I hope that I have shown that it is only by investigation of the fine details that the natural history of any species can be fully understood. This is the intellectual fascination of natural history, which so satisfactorily complements and justifies—if one needs to justify—one's enjoyment of the pursuit of it. Whether a bird lays two eggs or three; whether both parents feed the young or only the female; whether 10 percent or 20 percent of the nests succeed; whether 70 percent or 80 percent of the adults survive from one year to the next; each fact is significant, and all will be found to be interrelated.

II

The Future for the Cotingas

The future is not bright for the cotingas, nor is it for other creatures that depend on undisturbed tropical forest, which man is now destroying all over the world with frightening speed. But the situation is complex, ranging from disastrous in some areas to relatively good in others. The sort of sweeping generalizations that one reads in the more pessimistic newspaper and magazine articles cannot give a fair picture. One needs to know the facts firsthand in order to assess how real the danger is in any particular case, and it is very difficult for one person to know the facts for more than a few limited areas. I shall therefore attempt only a very summary account of the situation as I see it.

Unfortunately the idea of extinction of species has become so commonplace that many people unthinkingly accept the possibility that a bird or other animal is now extinct or soon will be. I blame the more sensational kind of popularization for this. One continually hears people asking "Is it extinct?" as they look at museum specimens of birds that are in fact alive and flourishing; and some seem almost disappointed to hear that they are fortunately far from extinct, as though this makes them less interesting. William Beebe, who did so much to interest Americans in the natural world around them, expressed most vividly the finality of extinction, and I cannot do better than quote his words. "The beauty and genius of a work of art may be reconceived though its first material expression be destroyed; a vanished harmony may yet again inspire the composer; but when the last individual of a race of living things breathes no more, another heaven and another earth must pass before such a one can be again."

What are the facts at present? Up to now, only 95 species of birds, out of a world total of some 8,500 species, are known to have become extinct as a result of man's activities in historical times. Another 65 subspecies (geographical races, recognizably different from other populations of the species to which they belong) have become extinct. These figures are taken from the *Red Data Book*, the invaluable compilation prepared by the International Council for Bird Preservation and published by the International Union for Conservation of Nature. Analyzed by decades, the figures are as follows:

	Number of species becoming extinct	Number of subspecies becoming extinct
1601–1650	4	–
1651–1700	5	–
1701–1750	7	–
1751–1800	12	4
1801–1850	14	5
1851–1900	33	28
1901–1950	20	27
1951 to date	–	1

The great majority of the species which have become extinct have been birds of oceanic islands, where the natural vegetation can be, and often has been, drastically altered by man, mainly as a result of his thoughtless introduction of domestic and other exotic animals. The *Red Data Book* does not in fact list one bird of the tropical forest among the extinctions.

But these figures give no cause for complacency. I am

afraid they only mean that we have seen the first wave of extinctions brought about by modern man. The worst of this first wave has passed, but another much bigger one is approaching, and it may well cause the extinction of many more species and geographical races of birds than the first. It is mainly the birds of montane tropical and subtropical forest that will disappear. In fact the extinctions have almost certainly begun, but it is much more difficult to be sure that a forest bird has disappeared, whose distribution may not have been exactly known in the first place, than that a species of bird has disappeared from a small island.

Colombia has more species of birds than any other country in the world. There are, or were, 1,556 species, and many of them are divided into recognizably different geographical races. Here, at the northern end of the Andes, the mountains are split into three main chains, the Western, Central, and Eastern Cordillera. Separated from the Andes in the extreme north is the immense isolated massif of the Sierra Nevada de Santa Marta, and isolated to the east is the much smaller Sierra Macarena. The vast complexity of this region, with different kinds of forests at different altitudinal levels separated by mountains that rise above the tree line, has enabled an unrivaled wealth of species and subspecies to evolve. The isolation of local populations has been the key factor, and the immense richness of the vegetation has provided the birds and other animals with a wealth of opportunities for specialization. Now, before the full richness of this avifauna has been catalogued,[49] it has begun to disappear forever. Under the pressure of the expanding human population, and for short-term agricultural gain, the forests have totally disappeared from vast areas of Colombia, mainly at subtropical levels in the mountains. Bare, steep, eroded mountainsides and dry watercourses have replaced richly forested slopes with clear streams. Dr. Carlos Lehmann, who for years has championed the cause of conservation in Colombia almost single-handed, has gone so far as to suggest that perhaps 500 forms of birds (species and subspecies) have gone from Colombia.[50] Even if this estimate is unduly pessimistic, the fact that so expert an observer can even suggest a figure of this order brings homes the magnitude of the disaster. In Central America, where human population pressure is as bad as in Colombia or worse, the destruction of montane forest in some areas is almost as disastrous, and there are many local forms of birds which must be rapidly disappearing.

Another area where many species are in imminent danger is the coastal region of southeastern Brazil. This is an area of high rainfall, and was formerly clothed in tropical forest from sea level to the tops of all but the highest mountains. The coastal forest belt is comparatively narrow and is separated from the main Amazonian forest by more arid country inland. As a consequence of this isolation the southeast Brazilian populations of a large number of birds—and other animals— that have wide distributions in South America have evolved differences of varying degree from their relatives to the northwest, and are now considered to be distinct species or subspecies. In addition, a smaller number of very distinct forms have arisen in southeastern Brazil and apparently have never spread to any other part of the continent. The avifauna of the eastern Brazilian coastal region is thus extraordinarily rich in peculiar forms.

In a well-known entry in the diary that he kept on his voyage round the world, Charles Darwin described his impressions when he first set foot in this forest on landing at Bahia, his first port of call on the South American mainland. "Bahia, or San Salvador, Brazil, Feb. 29th—The day has passed delightfully. Delight itself, however, is a weak term to express the feelings of a naturalist who, for the first time, has wandered by himself in a Brazilian forest. The elegance of the grasses, the novelty of the parasitical plants, the beauty of the flowers, the glossy green of the foliage, but above all the general luxuriance of the vegetation, filled me with admiration. A most paradoxical mixture of sound and silence pervades the shady parts of the wood. The noise from the insects is so loud, that it may be heard even from a vessel anchored several hundred yards from the shore; yet within the recesses of the forest a universal silence appears to reign. To a person fond of natural history such a day as this brings with it a deeper pleasure than he can ever hope to experience again."

Today, one would have to go a very long way from the town of Salvador to find any undisturbed forest. The east coast has become the most heavily populated and industrialized part of Brazil, and the greater part of the lowland forest has vanished, from Bahia in the north to Rio Grande do Sul in the south. With it have gone the forest birds, remnants of which are just holding out in the pockets of forest that remain. Helmut Sick, the most experienced Brazilian ornithologist and curator of birds at the Museu Nacional in Rio de Janeiro, has listed forty-six species or subspecies which he considers to be in danger of extinction in Brazil.[51] About two-thirds of them are confined to the eastern coastal forests.

These three main areas where forest birds are in greatest danger—the Colombian Andes, Central America, and eastern Brazil—have three things in common: they are relatively restricted in extent, they contain a large number of species with even more restricted ranges, and they have a dense human population. The situation is quite different in the Amazon basin and the adjoining Orinoco and Guiana region to the north. Here the extent of the forest is vast, the birds mainly have extensive ranges, and the human population is still small. It is not surprising, therefore, that no bird species is definitely known to be threatened with extinction in this area. But the Brazilian government is rapidly opening up Amazonia, driving roads through the forests and encouraging farming. The prospect of what may happen if the main Amazonian forest is destroyed by uncontrolled exploitation is so alarming that not only ecologists but the general public are beginning to be concerned. There appears to be a possibility of fundamental atmospheric and climatic alteration over a vast area, perhaps affecting the whole world. If the whole of the forest were destroyed, the disappearance of the whole of the forest avifauna might pale into insignificance beside such a disaster. But fortunately this is hardly likely, as some forest reserves have already been established and others probably will be. The most likely outcome is that blocks of protected forest will remain, but the evolution of the avifauna as a whole will be hopelessly disrupted.

Practical conservation measures would be very difficult in

a region like Amazonia, where so many birds are so little known, even if one had the cooperation of enlightened and efficient governments. In the first place we often know too little about a species to tell whether it is really rare or whether it has simply escaped detection. Occasional new species are still being discovered. Others, previously known from only one area, are found hundreds of miles away, suggesting that they may in fact be quite widespread. Another difficulty is that almost nothing is known about migrations and other movements. Many birds are certainly very sedentary, but others are known, or suspected on more or less good evidence, to migrate considerable distances; while others may wander more randomly in search of special foods. A block of forest that may be satisfactory for a sedentary species may not ensure the survival of one that needs to migrate.

Even so, reserves are the best hope. Unfortunately they become more and more difficult to establish and make effective when the damage to the forest has gone too far, as in much of Colombia and parts of Central America, and governments are, to put it mildly, not as effective as they might be. In Amazonia, however, there should in principle be no difficulty in setting up a large number of huge reserves, before the rush for land for speculative and other purposes gets out of hand. If this could be done, and the governments of the countries concerned—Brazil, Colombia, Venezuela, Ecuador, Peru, and Bolivia—could jointly declare their intentions of keeping these reserves inviolate, we should be a good deal less unhappy about the future of the cotingas and all the other life which the forest supports. The integrity of the Amazonian forest would be lost, and its long, slow evolution would come to a halt. This is inevitable now in any case. But at least the great majority of the species that now exist might be saved.

It is not impossible for undisturbed forest to persist close to great centers of human population. Indeed, the denser the human population the more essential it may be to keep some of the forest inviolate. São Paulo in southeastern Brazil is now the eleventh largest city in the world. It has been growing at a phenomenal speed and sprawls over miles of undulating country, its great clusters of skyscrapers surrounded by vast tracts of monotonous suburbs. For such a place to survive, an immense amount of water is needed, and huge pipes bring it across country from reservoirs in the surrounding hills. One important pipe comes from a reservoir in the Boraceia Forest Reserve, some seventy miles to the south, between São Paulo and the sea. This part of the coastal range, the Serra do Mar, is one of the wettest areas in Brazil, but the Brazilian authorities are well aware that the rain alone will not assure their water supplies; the forest must also be there, to absorb the moisture, protect the ground, and so ensure an even and constant replenishment of the rivers and the reservoirs. The Boraceia Reserve extends over some 40,000 acres, covering the upper catchment area of two important rivers which rise in this area. The dripping forests, festooned with epiphytes, are rich in bird life; some 200 species have been recorded, and there are probably more to be found. Most of them can survive indefinitely within the reserve. It is inconceivable that the authorities of the State of São Paulo will ever allow this forest to be destroyed. And there are others like it elsewhere in Brazil. Between them, they should secure the future of a very large number of species of forest birds. What they cannot necessarily do, however, is safeguard those birds that must migrate or move long distances in search of food.

I have so far discussed the cotingas' future prospects without mentioning them at all, since their fate is bound up with that of the forest on which they depend. And I intentionally excluded the manakins from the chapter heading, not because I care less for them but because as a family they are more tolerant of secondary forest and disturbed habitats, so will not feel man's impact as severely as the larger cotingas. How, in fact, are the various cotinga species faring, and how are they likely to do in the next few decades?

According to the most recent classification the family consists of seventy-nine species.[52] Of these, six may be in danger of extinction.

Kinglet Calyptura. This tiny cotinga is known only from two localities in the southeast of Brazil, in the State of Rio de Janeiro. It has apparently not been found in this cen-

tury. In the absence of any knowledge of its habitat requirements or habits it is impossible to say whether man
has caused its decline. It is even possible, though I think
unlikely, that it is not so very rare but simply very difficult
to detect.

Banded Cotinga. Almost certainly in danger of extinction.
Confined to the southeast Brazilian lowland tropical forest
which has now largely disappeared.

White-winged Cotinga. Situation almost exactly as for the
Banded Cotinga. These two species are the southeastern
Brazilian representatives of genera with wide distributions
in northern South America. As a result of long isolation in
the Brazilian coastal forests they have diverged sufficiently
from their relatives to be considered separate species.

Crimson Fruit-crow. One of the most remarkable of the
cotingas; a large, heavy bird with the plumage (in the male)
almost entirely deep crimson and with a glossy surface texture. It has been found in a small number of places in the
State of Pará in northern Brazil, and in the ninteenth
century and early in this century was recorded from the
Guianas. Sick considers its survival in Brazil threatened by
the construction of the new Belém-Brasilia road, which has
opened up the one area of forest where it is still known to
occur.

Long-wattled Umbrella-bird. Confined to the forests of the
Pacific slopes of the Andes in southwestern Colombia and
Ecuador. Destruction and disturbance of these forests make
the survival of this very large cotinga precarious unless adequate reserves can be set aside in time.

Bare-throated Umbrella-bird. Confined to mountain forests
in Costa Rica and Panama. Its situation is much the same as
for the preceding species. Fortunately, the Amazonian
Umbrella-bird, the third member of the group, has a wide
range in the Amazonian forests and can hardly be in danger
at present.

For millions of years the tropical forests and the animals within them have undergone a slow evolution. The forests have increased in extent and contracted, slowly shifting their boundaries as climates have become wetter or drier, warmer or cooler. The trees and smaller plants have multiplied in number of species, evolving diverse adaptations in their growth forms, flowers, and fruits. The birds and other animals have become finely adapted to exploiting the varied resources of the forest; and they too have multiplied in number of species, as populations have become isolated from one another by rivers, seas, or open country, have undergone divergent evolutionary changes in isolation and then, on the breaking down of these barriers, have invaded each others' ranges. As new species have risen others have become extinct; but the process has been gradual until the arrival of man. It is probable that the richness and complexity of the forest was steadily increasing.

In the tropical forests of the New World, man appeared on the scene only a few thousand years ago. He hunted some birds, fished, and cleared and cultivated small patches of ground, but he made very little impact on the forest. He accumulated a great deal of knowledge about the forest animals, but none of this reached the outside world. It was only about 150 years ago that western man began a thorough exploration of the forest. The collecting and cataloguing of the birds began. In the exciting decades of the second half of the nineteenth century the extraordinary richness of the avifauna became apparent. New species were continually being discovered; systematic ornithologists were busy examining and describing them, while the anatomists dissected them and tried to work out the relationships of the strange new types by comparing their internal structures. By the end of the century most of the species had been discovered; but even today the list is not complete. As recently as 1965, for instance, a new cotinga was discovered in eastern Peru, so distinct from all other members of the family that it has been placed in a new genus.

The cataloguing stage is nearly over, but the more interesting second stage, the study of the birds in life, has only just begun. No detailed field studies of individual species were made until the 1920s. The greatest pioneer in the field study of tropical American birds, Alexander Skutch, is still actively at work. The special tragedy, from our selfish and limited point of view, is that just as the wealth is being revealed to us it is being destroyed, and much of it will soon be irretrievably lost. But I do not think that our concern is wholly selfish. The disaster will continue to affect the lives of all our descendants, though its impact will be blunted, for one cannot feel very strongly the lack of what one has never known.[53] How complete and devastating the disaster will be will be decided in the next few decades. I should like to think that my great-grandchildren, if I have any, will be able to walk up the Arima Valley in Trinidad and hear the bellbirds calling and see toucans flying from treetop to treetop, or, if they are more adventurous, will be able to search for and find the Crimson Fruit-crow in the forests of the Guianas.

Notes

(Numbered according to the small superior numbers in the text)

1. For a full account of the Bearded Bellbird, see B. K. Snow 1970, "A Field Study of the Bearded Bellbird in Trinidad"; *Ibis* 112: 299–239. For a general account of all the bellbirds, see D. W. Snow 1973, Distribution, Ecology and Evolution of the Bellbirds (*Procnias*, Cotingidae); *Bull. Br. Mus. Nat. Hist. (Zool.)* 25: 369–391.

2. Most birds undergo a complete molt after breeding. In Trinidad, at 10° N, the molt season for most birds is much the same as it is in Britain, being at its height in the months July–September.

3. This subject has recently been dealt with in a fascinating book by Crawford H. Greenewalt, *Bird song: acoustics and physiology* (Washington, Smithsonian Institution Press, 1968).

   Birds produce their calls by means of resonating membranes in the wall of the syrinx, a cartilaginous structure at the junction where the two bronchi from the lungs unite to form the trachea. There is apparently, at least in most birds, little or no modulation of the sound in the trachea or mouth cavity. The syrinx of songbirds has extrinsic muscles (muscles connecting the syrinx with adjacent structures) and intrinsic muscles (muscles connecting different parts of the syrinx). Primitive songbirds such as cotingas and manakins have a simpler arrangement of intrinsic muscles than the more advanced songbirds, such as thrushes and finches, and cannot utter such varied and complex songs. The mechanics of sound production in the syrinx is not understood in detail; but it is known that a high air pressure must be maintained in the air sacs surrounding the syrinx, otherwise no sound can be produced. The loudness of the sound that can be uttered varies with the surrounding air pressure, and so birds like the bellbirds that utter extraordinarily loud, explosive calls must build up a very high pressure in the air sacs surrounding the syrinx.

4. A. F. Skutch 1969. "Life Histories of Central American Birds III"; *Pacific Coast Avifauna,* 35 (Cooper Ornithological Society).

5. *Bird Songs from the Tropics,* recorded and produced by Paul Schwartz, Instituto Neotropical, Apartado 4640, Caracas, Venezuela.

6. The postage stamp issued by Ecuador in 1959 shows a Cock-of-the-rock perched on a bare rock against a background of mountains, thus following the old tradition. The stamp issued by Guyana in 1966 avoids this mistake, but the bird depicted is the Andean Cock-of-the-rock, which is not found nearer than about 1,000 miles from Guyana.

7. W. Frost 1910, The Cock-of-the-rock; *Avic. Mag.* 3: 319–324.

8. Gilliard's account is published in *Bull. Am. Mus. Nat. Hist.* 124 (1962): 31–68. A popular account of his expedition is given in the *National Geographic Magazine* vol. 121 (January 1962).

9. For a fuller account of these observations, see D. W. Snow 1971, Notes on the Biology of the Cock-of-the-rock; *J. Orn. Lpz.* 112: 323–333.

10. The two most dangerous poisonous snakes, the fer-de-lance and the bushmaster, are widespread in tropical American forests, but they are seldom seen by day. William's experience was unusual, though there is a general belief that the fer-de-lance is more apt to strike without provocation than the bushmaster. Antivenin can now be obtained in dehydrated form and it is a wise safeguard to take a supply if one is going to camp beyond immediate reach of a hospital; but if one takes a few precautions, such as not walking about at night without a good torch, it is most unlikely that it will ever have to be used. The more urbanized inhabitants of Trinidad and

Guyana have an absurd fear of snakes and many will hardly dare to walk a step in the forest. This would not matter very much if it were not for the fact that it contributes to the general feeling that the forest is dangerous and best cleared as soon as possible.

11. For a full account of this work see D. W. Snow 1962, A Field Study of the Black-and-white Manakin, *Manacus manacus,* in Trinidad; *Zoologica N.Y.* 47: 65–104.

12. Chapman's account is published in *Bull. Am. Mus. Nat. Hist.* 68 (1935): 471–525.

13. See P. R. Lowe 1942, The Anatomy of Gould's Manakin (*Manacus vitellinus*) in Relation to its Display; *Ibis* (14) 6: 50–83.

14. Ornithologists will not need an explanatory note on mist-nets, but other readers may. Originally developed in Japan and used commercially for bird catching, mist-nets are now perhaps the most important means of trapping birds for scientific study. They are very fine nets made of black nylon (in Japan, originally of silk), with a small number of tighter and thicker horizontal strands threaded through the meshes at intervals, dividing the net into a number of partitions or "shelves." Against a dark background mist-nets are almost invisible and birds simply fly into them without being aware that they are there. When a bird flies into the loose net, its impetus carries it forward until it falls and is then trapped in a pocket of net behind one of the tight shelf strings. It hangs there helplessly but unharmed until extracted.

15. These and other longevity records are given in D. W. Snow and A. Lill 1974, Longevity records for some neotropical land birds; *Condor* 76: 262–267.

16. For a full account of these Tobago observations, see D. W. Snow 1963, The display of the Blue-backed Manakin, *Chiroxiphia pareola,* in Tobago, W.I.; *Zoologica N.Y.* 48: 167–176.

17. See D. W. Snow 1971, Social organization of the Blue-backed Manakin; *Wilson Bull.* 83: 35–38.

18. Bird songs and calls are now regularly studied and analyzed by means of a machine called a sound spectrograph or sona-graph, which produces a visual representation of the sound known as a sound spectrogram or sonagram. A sound spectrogram is a two-dimensional trace in which the vertical scale

represents the frequency, or pitch, of the sound and the horizontal scale represents time. Thus a pure note with a rising inflection might look something like this:

The Blue-backed Manakin's "chup," a note with a sharp beginning and a wide range of frequencies, looks like this:

and the "chups" of two birds calling in unison appear like this:

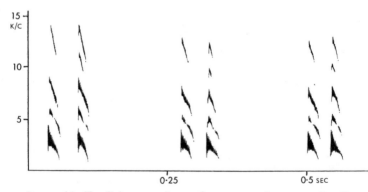

19. I use this English name in preference to the name Swallow-tailed Manakin, used in recent handbooks of South American birds. The latter is an example of a wholly inappropriate name imposed on the bird by ornithologists. The bird's tail is nothing like a swallow's. The central pair of tail feathers are

elongated, like a bee-eater's, whereas a swallow's tail is of the opposite shape, with the outer feathers prolonged. The predominantly blue body of the male, unique in a manakin, makes the name Blue Manakin quite appropriate, and incidentally echoes the name of one of the most remarkable counterparts of the cotingas and manakins in the Old World, the Blue Bird of Paradise.

20. E. G. Holt 1925, The dance of the Tangará (*Chiroxiphia caudata* (Shaw)); *Auk* 42: 588–590. H. Sick 1959, Die Balz der Schmuckvögel (Pipridae); *J. Orn. Lpz.* 100: 269–302. Of all the published accounts, Holt's agrees most closely with our own observations. In his account (also given in English in *The Living Bird* 6 (1967): 5–22) Sick erroneously describes the bird at the far end of the line as jumping up and moving forward in the air to the front of the queue, thus reversing the rotation of the Catherine wheel.

21. These arguments are developed more fully in D. W. Snow 1971, Evolutionary aspects of fruit-eating by birds; *Ibis* 113: 194–202.

22. The number of species in these families is still a matter for further research. Certainly all but a very few of the existing species have been discovered, but there is still uncertainty in many cases as to whether closely related forms which replace one another geographically should be considered to belong to the same or to different species. The figures given here are taken from Van Tyne & Berger's *Fundamentals of Ornithology* (1959), except for the cotingas, for which the number of species is based on my own assessment.

23. Analyses of the pericarps (fleshy parts) of several kinds of fruits eaten by specialized fruit-eating birds in Trinidad showed that proteins made up 5–14 percent (average 11 percent) of the dry weight, and fats 19–39 percent (average 31 percent) of the dry weight. For succulent fruits the equivalent figures were 2–6 percent for proteins and a trace (less than 1 percent) for fats. Moreover, the pericarps of palms, laurels, and other very nutritious fruits contain far less water than the pericarps of succulent fruits.

24. The ornithologists in the tropical forest is very fortunate compared with the botanist. Because the number of bird species is comparatively small and their distribution and classification is fairly well known, there is usually no difficulty in knowing what birds one is dealing with, and one can usually go

straight on to the next and more interesting stage, the investigation of their behavior and ecology. For the botanist, on the other hand, the complexity of the flora is such that he must spend most of his time collecting and then trying to work out the identity of his plants, a highly technical process the results of which can hardly be appreciated except by a fellow botanist.

25. Alfred Russel Wallace, who found the key to evolution in natural selection at the same time as Darwin and worked out many of the implications of their joint discovery, remained completely unconvinced by Darwin's theory of sexual selection except insofar as it concerned horns, tusks, and the other characteristics by which males compete directly among themselves for females. The lack of any real evidence that females prefer the best adorned males led him to suggest that highly developed display plumage and other adornments are the direct result of excessive nervous and muscular activity in particular areas of the body surface—a theory that is open to far more damaging criticism than Darwin's.

26. See A. Lill 1974. Sexual behavior of the lek-forming White-bearded Manakin (*Manacus manacus trinitatis* Hartert). Z. *Tierpsychol.* 36: 1–36.

27. See A. J. Hogan-Warburg 1966, Social behavior of the Ruff, *Philmachus pugnax* (L.); *Ardea* 54: 109–229. This remarkable study shows that the Ruff has other complexities in addition to the variability of individual males. The males are of two distinct types: the court-holding males, which show well-developed aggressive behavior and have mainly dark head plumes; and the "satellite" males, which are quite without aggressive behavior, do not own any courts, and have mainly white head plumes. The satellite males are tolerated at their courts by the owning males and may, in fact, be equally successful in mating. There is no known parallel to this dichotomy of plumage and behavior in any other species of bird.

28. See B. K. Snow 1972, A field study of the Calfbird *Perissocephalus tricolor; Ibis* 114: 139–162.

29. See E. O. Willis 1973, The behavior of Ocellated Antbirds; *Smiths. Contr. Zool.* 144.

30. It is a general phenomenon that there are fewer species of animals on islands than on comparable areas of mainland, and that those that do occur are more abundant. The reason for

the number of species on islands has been debated. The reason for the greater abundance of those species that are present is presumably that island species occupy a wider range of ecological "niches," which may be shared between several species on the mainland, and so can exist at a level of abundance equivalent to the combined abundance of those species on the mainland. Trinidad has fewer bird species than the adjacent mainland, and this may be part of the reason for the abundance of some of the forest species; but a more important factor, in the part of the Arima Valley where we worked, was probably the suitability of the habitat. For the manakins the area provided a particularly rich food supply; the forest was broken up and intersected by paths and streams, with a main road running up the valley, giving great scope for melastomes and other berry-bearing plants that colonize forest edges and open spaces.

31. W. Beebe 1924, The rarest of nests in the tallest of grass stems; *Bull. N.Y. Zool. Soc.* 27: 114–117.

32. A. F. Skutch 1968, The cotingas: a study in contrasts; *Animal Kingdom* 73: 5–9.

33. A bird which has suffered from the attempts to give it an English name. The scientific name, which cannot be changed, is *Pipromorpha oleaginea* (referring to its supposed manakin-like shape and the "oily," in fact olive green, color of its upperparts). From this it temporarily acquired the English name Oleaginous Pipromorpha. Realizing that such a name could hardly come into general use, some later authors made an effort to find something shorter but their choice, Oily Flycatcher, merely lost the quaintness of the former name without being much more appropriate. The name now used in the most recent handbooks, Ochre-bellied Flycatcher, refers to the color of the under parts. Though unobjectionable, like so many of these recently coined names, it lacks inspiration.

34. In tropical forests, where downpours are frequent and torrential, nests must be proof against getting soaked—or at least proof against getting sodden as a result of being soaked. Some covered nests have a thatch which deflects the rain; but for most nests the solution is simply to be made of materials that dry out quickly and do not become sodden. Hummingbird nests and some others, which incorporate vegetable down and other cottony materials which would

become sodden, are covered on the outside with lichens and cobwebs and other materials that form a more or less waterproof coat. In the case of open nests, the parent bird must of course be sitting if the contents of the nest cup are to remain dry. An incidental advantage of the very small stick nests built by the cotingas is that the parent can keep both nest and contents completely dry by completely covering both of them.

35. The most abundant hummingbirds in the interior of the forest, where they feed and nest close to the ground. They apparently get their name from their sober plumage, consisting mainly of browns, olives, and grays, which is in striking contrast to the brilliant iridescent colors of most other hummingbirds. In other respects the name is not appropriate, for the "hermits" are a prime example of nectar-eating birds whose social organization parallels that of the fruit-eaters discussed in this book. The males spend the greater part of their time singing and displaying in groups, each bird maintaining its own small territory of a few square yards within the lek. The females visit the lek to mate, and undertake all nesting duties single-handed. This at least is the general pattern, from which a few species of hermits depart to some extent.

36. Helmut Sick (1957, *J. Orn. Lpz.* 98: 421–31) has given a full account of how he first established the identity of this remarkable nest material. In Brazil, where his observations were made, some birds build their nests either of *Marasmius* or of strands of "Spanish moss" (*Tillandsia usneoides*), an epiphytic bromeliad which festoons trees in very humid areas. Where both *Marasmius* and *Tillandsia* occur, in the wet coastal mountains of eastern Brazil, *Tillandsia* may be the preferred material; but in central Brazil, where it is too dry for *Tillandsia* to grow, *Marasmius* only is used.

37. See B. K. Snow 1974, Lek behaviour and breeding of Guy's Hermit Hummingbird *Phaethornis guy; Ibis* 116: 278–297.

38. Y. Willis, personal communication.

39. See D. R. Griffin 1953, Acoustic orientation in the Oilbird, *Steatornis; Proc. Nat. Acad. Sci.* 39: 884–893.

40. In 1966 the estate was purchased with money donated mainly from the U.S.A., with a substantial contribution from the United Kingdom, and was established as a nature reserve, the first of its kind in the West Indies. The estate house was en-

larged and converted into a guesthouse. The Asa Wright Nature Centre, as it is called, is now run by a board of management consisting of Trinidad and overseas members in equal numbers. It has become increasingly well known as one of the finest places for beginning to learn the richness of the American tropical forest avifauna.

41. The results of these studies are contained in D. W. Snow 1961–62, The natural history of the Oilbird, *Steatornis caripensis; Zoologica N.Y.* 46: 27–48; 47: 199–221.

42. See C. G. Sibley 1960, The electrophoretic patterns of avian egg-white proteins as taxonomic characters; *Ibis* 102: 215–259.

43. All bright red, orange, and yellow colors in birds are produced by a group of pigments known as carotenoids (also as lipochromes, as they are soluble in fats, or lipids). As far as is known, no vertebrate animal can synthesize carotenoids. Several kinds of carotenoids have been described, one of which, cotingin, has been found only in the plumage of some cotingas. A peculiar property of the very dark red or purple red feathers of these cotingas is that if they are heated their color pales and changes to orange red; and more surprisingly, mechanical pressure can have the same effect. Collectors working in humid tropical forests have sometimes had to dry their bird skins over a fire, which does not matter for most specimens; but discolored patches on the red cotingas sometimes show that they have been dried too close to the flames.

44. See A. F. Skutch 1949, Do tropical birds rear as many young as they can nourish?; *Ibis* 91: 430–455.

45. See D. W. Snow 1971, Observations on the Purple-throated Fruit-crow in Guyana; *Living Bird* 10: 5–17. I have not included this bird among the cotingas described in detail in this book because it is not a specialized fruit-eater. Insects are as important as fruit in its diet, and it feeds its young mainly on insects. Many tropical birds, from a number of different families, have evolved a social organization in which the unit is a closely knit group of several adults. The members of a group not only feed and roost together but jointly attend a single nest. Much more field work needs to be done before this habit can be properly understood; it would certainly provide a theme every bit as fascinating as the interaction between birds and fruits.

46. See D. W. Snow 1962, Notes on the biology of some Trinidad swifts; *Zoologica N.Y.* 47: 129–139.
47. This view is associated with the late Dr. David Lack, Director of the Edward Grey Institute of Field Ornithology at Oxford. It was first fully developed in his book *The natural regulation of animal numbers* (1954).
48. This view is closely associated with Professor V. C. Wynne-Edwards, who set it out very fully in his book *Animal dispersion in relation to social behaviour* (1962). It is also the "common sense" view that has usually been adopted by naturalists who have not had to reconcile it with what is known of the working of natural selection.
49. As recently as 1966 a new species of hummingbird was discovered on the west slope of the Western Andes in southern Colombia. The scientific name is *Eriocnemis mirabilis;* the generic name refers to the woollike tufts of white feathers at the base of the legs, and the specific name to the wonder and surprise of finding it in an area that has been well worked by collectors. "Colorful puffleg" is the inadequate English name adopted by the handbooks.
50. F. C. Lehmann 1970, Avifauna of Colombia, in *The avifauna of northern Latin America* (Washington, Smithsonian Institution Press).
51. H. Sick 1969, Aves brasileiras ameaçadas de extinção e noções gerais de conservação de aves no Brasil; *An. Acad. brasil. Cienc.* 41: 205–229.
52. D. W. Snow 1973, The classification of the Cotingidae; *Breviora* No. 409.
53. In his monumental work *The bird faunas of Africa and its islands* (Academic Press, New York and London, 1966) the late R. E. Moreau included in his Foreword the following passage, which could equally well apply to South America: "I am sure that relatively small parts of Africa will remain much as they are for a long time; but I am also aware that, if things go for the Africans as many of them and of their friends would wish, they will in a few years and over most of the continent have hunted and burned and cultivated and built and procreated themselves out of any semblance of their natural *oikos* as thoroughly as the people of the Lower Yangtse, or the cornlands of the Middle West, or the Cyclades, or the shore-line of Sussex. By the time the Africans are ready to become amateurs of field biology most of them

will have to scrabble about in the ruins of their fauna and flora, as everybody else in a 'developed' country must do; and instead of studying the grand designs of natural biomes they will have to finick around with the impoverished and lopsided remnants which are the by-products of man's multiple incontinencies."

Appendix

Scientific names of the birds mentioned in this book

Andean Cock-of-the-rock	*Rupicola peruviana*
Andean Hill-star	*Oreotrochilus estella*
Banded Cotinga	*Cotinga maculata*
Bare-throated Bellbird	*Procnias nudicollis*
Bare-throated Umbrella-bird	*Cephalopterus glabricollis*
Bearded Bellbird	*Procnias averano*
Black-and-white Manakin	*Manacus manacus*
Blackbird	*Turdus merula*
Black Curassow	*Crax alector*
Black Grouse	*Lyrurus tetrix*
Black-headed Gull	*Larus ridibundus*
Blue-backed Manakin	*Chiroxiphia pareola*
Blue Jay	*Cyanocitta cristata*
Blue Manakin	*Chiroxiphia caudata*
Calfbird	*Perissocephalus tricolor*
Carrion Crow	*Corvus corone*
Chestnut-collared Swift	*Cypseloides rutilus*
Chimney Swift	*Chaetura pelagica*
Cock-of-the-rock	*Rupicola rupicola*
Crimson Fruit-crow	*Haematoderus militaris*
Dunnock	*Prunella modularis*
Golden-headed Manakin	*Pipra erythrocephala*

Golden Pheasant	*Chrysolophus pictus*
Gould's Manakin	*Manacus manacus vitellinus*
Guy's Hermit	*Phaethornis guy*
Hairy Hermit	*Glaucis hirsuta*
Harpy Eagle	*Harpia harpyja*
Herring Gull	*Larus argentatus*
Hooded Berry-eater	*Carpornis cucullatus*
House Sparrow	*Passer domesticus*
Kinglet Calyptura	*Calyptura cristata*
Long-wattled Umbrella-bird	*Cephalopterus penduliger*
Ocellated Antbird	*Phaenostictus mcleannani*
Oilbird	*Steatornis caripensis*
Ovenbird	*Furnarius rufus*
Peacock	*Pavo cristatus*
Pipromorpha	*Pipromorpha oleaginea*
Pompadour Cotinga	*Xipholena punicea*
Purple-throated Fruit-crow	*Querula purpurata*
Ruff	*Philomachus pugnax*
Rufus Piha	*Lipaugus unirufus*
Short-tailed Swift	*Chaetura brachyura*
Shrike-like Cotinga	*Laniisoma elegans*
Slaty-capped Flycatcher	*Leptopogon superciliaris*
Song Thrush	*Turdus philomelos*
Three-wattled Bellbird	*Procnias tricarunculata*
White Bellbird	*Procnias alba*
White-winged Cotinga	*Xipholena atropurpurea*
Wren	*Trogodytes troglodytes*